FROM THE MIND OF CRITIC 2017

BRYAN RADZIN

FROM THE MIND OF CRITIC 2017

© 2018 LULU, ALL RIGHTS RESERVED

ISBN# 978-0-578-20735-3

UNRELENTING POSITIVITY

AUTHOR: BRYAN RADZIN

COVER PHOTOS: BRYAN RADZIN

I DEDICATE THIS TO ALL THOSE WHO MAY NOT SEE THE LIGHT AT THE END OF THE TUNNEL, BUT MOVE FORWARD ANYWAY BECAUSE THEY FEEL IT IN THEIR SOUL.

ACKNOWLEDGMENTS

Thank you Mom for the love and support my soul requires to survive. I hope with the publication of this my 11th book, that it leads me to make a living spreading truth through love, humanism and accountability by following the synchronicities I feel from the bottom of my soul. Thank you Pop for teaching me to take everything with a grain of salt, and to always ask why; it is that ability which you have ingrained in my psyche, which will make me not only a famous writer, but an informed citizen of the world who has a chance to serve his true purpose.

Thank you Laurie for helping me take my dad's lessons a step further in my personal evolution, and for being the utter definition of not only a true friend, but an authentic, loving and purposeful human being. Thank you for Tim for being my brother, my comrade in arms, my personal Kenny Powers, and the one guy who can make me laugh, think and feel loved all in the same breath.

Thank you Ryan for being my brother and always pushing me to become bigger and better than I thought possible. I don't think there is anybody id rather share a beer with, or watch a football game with. One day we'll be enjoy beer you've made with food I've made, and it will change the world when we become millionaires off it.

Thank you to the Arcata Marsh, the Mad River, The Fieldbrook Loop and The Maple Creek Loop for providing not only peace of mind and uplifting energy when I'm low, but for imprinting on my brain what a slower, and more authentic way of life is all about. As the world gets bigger, faster and more intense with each passing day, it's these natural treasures I take advantage of which not only remind me what makes life worth living and what real beauty is, but also to fill my cup as often as possible, specifically so I can fill the cups of others. Thank you world for the opportunity, I'm eternally grateful ☺☺☺☺

PROLOGUE

If we see not light at the end of the tunnel, but specks of light throughout, is there a way to meld these specks together so they specifically illuminate our personal path forward? Can we stay focused on what's important, while staying focused on what brings us joy? Are they one in the same, symbiotic or diametrically opposed to each other? Does our path forward clash in direct opposition with other paths, creating a chaotic soup of humanity that throws our priorities all out of whack, by making us believe a finite number of paths exist? We all are struggling to survive, live, love and prosper. This adversity ingrained in us as human beings on planet earth in the 21st century, is enabled by social status, materialism and organizations which espouse easy answers and salvation, but only vacuum up wallets and critically thinking minds. The biggest thing we can do for ourselves, is remembering what makes us human is what makes life beautiful, because what makes us different makes us the same. We all go through dark tunnels, knowing we must trudge through to reach light at the end. We might not be able to force slivers of light along our journey to combine, but we can make them more frequent, by recognizing them and letting them go. Darkness may feel so overpowering it seems destined to engulf everything good and just. This is an illusion, which will be vivisected once we allow our personal roadblocks to crumble under the world's beauty.

FROM THE MIND OF CRITIC
JANUARY 3RD 2017

From the mind of critic: "If resolutions are meant to guide us through the coming year by improving our lives and bringing us joy, why do we forget them so quickly? Do we believe voicing the words is enough, thinking it's the only effort we must exert? Are we scared improving ourselves entails changing who we are, and we'd rather stay the same, even if it means stagnation? Many of us believe the new year provides a fresh start, a clean slate to engineer each and everything we want to see happen. Some of us are more ambitious than others, but we all want to be successful at what we attempt. We run into trouble when we lay out elaborate ideas, but neglect to lay a foundation to make them possible. Maybe this is a symptom of a bigger disease. Maybe it has become so imbedded in our political system, that no matter what end of the spectrum we find ourselves on, we're really good at articulating problems, but fail to articulate solutions. Our political leaders learn this concept from us, because they are us. Whether it's a resolution or venting political opinion, we must follow through. We must walk the walk and do what we say, or nobody will believe what anybody says, and nothing will change. We must ask ourselves if we want to make positive change, or just say we do." ☺

FROM THE MIND OF CRITIC
JANUARY 4TH 2017

From the mind of critic: "If the key to life is defining happiness, which we find by awakening inner joy, do we only need ourselves? If feeding inner joy is how we find purpose, are we really an island? Do we need others to define us, or do we need to define ourselves? There's no question, we're the people we've been looking for. We must be the change we want to see. Issues arise when we think we don't need anybody, and that everything is on us if we want to succeed, evolve and move forward. This can be extremely motivating when achieving our goals, but is tough when we share with somebody emotionally or physically. This act of sharing is not done to define our inner joy, but to expand and enhance it. This not only lifts our inner joy, but helps others lift theirs. We share our experiences and lift their inner joy. They share their experiences and lift our inner joy. Once we realize that this balanced back and forth is the key to the whole equation, we'll see that we define our inner joy, and others bring it to life. It's like reading books about something, then experiencing that same thing in real life. We need full knowledge, before understanding is reached. Our inner joy is up to us, and under our control. Bringing that inner joy to life, is up to the people we choose to surround ourselves with." ☺

FROM THE MIND OF CRITIC
JANUARY 5TH 2017

From the mind of critic: "If things have to get worse before they get better, is it because some of us are slow? Do we think some problems aren't very bad, and don't require solutions unless they're personally and forcefully slapping us in the face? Do we see the problem as so big, imbedded and generationally powerful, that we also fail to act unless it personally slaps us in the face? Have we let problems fester because we've been searching for the perfect solution, and won't settle for anything less? Problems arise at different times for different reasons. Our life experience guides the direction of our action or inaction. Have our biases and pre-conceived notions grown so strong, that if we hear anything that pokes through our bias created armor, we feel threatened and become more entrenched? Whatever stage we're at of viewing big picture problems, we could all agree the next few years will be very interesting. Every extreme thought, feeling and action ever dreamed, will be thrown on the table; half the government, gone. Medicaid, Medicare and Social Security gone. Food stamps, financial assistance and public education gone; Environmental protections, diplomacy and regulations on everything from food to taxes, gone. I'm not saying all these things will happen, but I guarantee each one will be attempted. We must do something, anything, unless we want America as a concept to no longer exist." ☺

FROM THE MIND OF CRITIC

JANUARY 6TH 2017

From the mind of critic: "Does one plus one always equal two, or does it sometimes equal one? Does bringing two things together always keep them separate entities, unable to combine because of similarities? Can two separate entities combine to make one, coalescing around similarities, balancing each other out around differences? We all come from different backgrounds, cultures, upbringings, environments, religions, and political belief structures. However, we also come from the same human beginnings, because we strive for the same basic things, by wanting love, peace, security, and to make a difference. When so many of us are currently at each other's throats, it seems we'll never unite to create the critical mass needed to affect collective positive change. It seems we're so different, and are being pulled away from the positive gains we've made as a community. However, once we realize we're happier, more prosperous and more productive when all of us are, we'll see dividing people into different groups because they believe differently, doesn't mean they're threatening us, it means we're threatening ourselves. One plus one does equal one, when we see ourselves as equals. This isn't math, it's the future construct of our species.

Separate but equal never is and never was equal, equal is equal because it's equal. We will unite, when we truly see. We must add to each other, not subtract." ☺

FROM THE MIND OF CRITIC

JANUARY 7TH 2017

From the mind of critic: "If money is the root of all evil, is having all the money in the world a better determining factor of our inherent character, then if we had no money? Would we portray the most honest version of ourselves, if we could do whatever we wanted? Would a more honest version be portrayed, if we had no means to do anything? Rhetorical questions and exercises help prepare us for all sorts of life situations. This is especially true when determining what kind of person we are, and what kind of person we'd like to be. Do we want to be honest and trustworthy, or liars and unreliable? Would we make decisions that benefit humanity and the planet, if we could buy and sell everybody and everything, by moving pieces around so the system works better for everyone, no matter what we look like, what we believe or who we choose to love? Would we make decisions for the good of humanity if we relied on personal interactions, to show people a balance of tolerance, acceptance, love, kindness, and the courage to overcome adversity to make dreams come true? Would these people we come into contact feel compelled to spread these thoughts to everybody they come into contact with? Once we realize money or the lack there of isn't a character determinant, we'll see the only true measure is kindness to ourselves and others. We just have to ask ourselves how we'd like to be treated." ☺

FROM THE MIND OF CRITIC
JANUARY 11TH 2017

From the mind of critic: "If we express ourselves and people feel we're attacking them, does it prevent us from being honest? Does viewing our words, body language and tone differently than the person we're directing it toward, make it seem like we're being attacked because people view things differently? Somewhere in our subconscious do we know we're attacking the person, only because we feel attacked? We hit somebody, they hit us back, then we hit them again, and on and on it goes. What may start out as one person calmly expressing how they feel or what they think, can quickly blow up into a continuous tit for tat. Maybe we don't have the capacity to step into another person's shoes. Maybe we can't fathom how language sounds normal to us, but to another it feels like they're being attacked. Then in an effort to defend themselves, they attack us. Then in an effort to defend ourselves, we attack them. Then the whole thing gets completely blown out of proportion, when it should have stayed a judgment free zone by having an honest back and forth. Many things anger us from family, to politics to the world. Once we realize we can't express ourselves honestly when we're angry because we can't think straight, we'll see that to diffuse a situation we must stay cool, calm and collected. If we ever want to get past our ingrained issues, we have to have honest discussion.

To have honest discussion, we can't fly off the handle when honesty is displayed. Honesty is the best policy in any relationship. However, unless we let honesty flow without attacking it, we'll never get where we want to go. We let honesty in, by not erecting road blocks." ☺

FROM THE MIND OF CRITIC
JANUARY 12TH 2017

From the mind of critic: "If all of us recognize and accept truth at varying degrees, how long do we have to wait for positive change? Will we go so far down the rabbit-hole, that by the time we see how corrupt, dishonest and fascist our government has become, it'll be too late? Will slivers of light continue to flicker, until their frequency and illumination become such a big part of our daily life, we wonder how we stepped down the rabbit hole in the first place? What most of us see as corruption, criminality and outright flouting of the constitution, others see as creating a new way of life. All of us will be tested in the next year, to see if we care about government officials personally profiting off of not only the offices they hold, but the decisions they make. Do we even want to protect the environment? Do we need to regulate taxes at all? Do we want to give people free education, or believe they're entitled to an education or health care as fundamental? What about supporting the poor, or do we only support the rich because we believe the fallacy that we all can become rich? Have we drunk the Kool-Aid that says billionaires will spend more money if we give them more money? It's not about being left or right, democrat or republican, liberal or conservative. It's about criminals, corruption, money and destruction. Do we want to see the complete destruction of the American experiment, where we no longer remember what it was like to be free?

Will we stand up and fight for what we believe, making sure all American usurpers about to take office are swept into the dustbin of history? We have until January 20th to figure it out." ☺

FROM THE MIND OF CRITIC

JANUARY 13TH 2017

From the mind of critic: "If conflicts of interest are the very foundation of corruption, and we agree corruption is bad no matter what side of the political spectrum we're on, will we stand up and stop it when its authenticity is undeniable? If somebody bounces back and forth between politics and business, governing the same things they profited on, before returning to profit on them again, is that corruption? If somebody continues to profit off business ventures when they're in office, but does so through back channels because they don't want the public to know, is that corruption? If somebody not only profits while in office, but does it so openly and unapologetically that their name is on the building, while charging the secret service to protect them, and having money roll in from foreign governments because of services rendered, is that corruption? Will we be blinded by all the racism, sexism and lying meant to obscure that corruption? I would say we're entering a whole new era on January 20th, but anybody paying attention would know that's not true. All of this has happened before. We're witnessing the natural evolution of everything swept under the rug. Well the rug has not only been pulled up but burned, spreading its ashes all over the country. Will we admit corruption exists in all people? Will we fight tooth and nail to stop it no matter where it lies?

Will we continue supporting corruption, because we see our side as able to get off scott-free? Facts and truth do matter, and they do exist. Will we stop lying to ourselves in time to see?" ☺

FROM THE MIND OF CRITIC

JANUARY 14TH 2017

From the mind of critic: "Do we believe in liberty and justice for all, that all men are created equal and that we all have the right to life, liberty and the pursuit of happiness, only if it pertains to us? Do we see violence, crime, wars, unrest and downright chaos, and believe all we can do is protect ourselves and people like us, because everyone else is out to get us? Do we live the old adage of being the change we want to see, by understanding that if we want equality, liberty, justice and joy for the nation as a whole, we have to start with every interaction we have? Will the people we interact with spread it to everyone they interact with and so on? As Americans we can be a very arrogant, narcissistic, self-centered, obnoxious and intolerant people. We can also be a very loving, caring, understanding, peaceful and accepting people. In the next year, and more likely the next six months all of that will be put to the test. Everything will be out in the open. All our darkest secrets and desires will be spread out on the table for the nation and the world to see. This could be the downfall of everything we thought we were as Americans, with every creepy, underhanded, hateful, racist radical coming out of the woodworks, because they see every department and cabinet position as finally supporting them.

However, this could finally be the fulfillment of the great American experiment, where every loving, courageous and die-hard peacemaker comes out of the woodworks, because they finally see an opportunity to put down the overt darkness in every department and cabinet position. Do we all want to be free, or do we want none of us to be free? Those are our only choices." ☺

FROM THE MIND OF CRITIC
JANUARY 18TH 2017

From the mind of critic: "If we get so shaken to our core that we start questioning our soul's motivation, how do we protect ourselves from being shaken again? Do we erect such a hardened wall, that neither light, love nor positive energy can provide the jackhammer needed to bust through? Do we build a bridge big enough so all the darkness, hate and negative energy provide the mac trucks needed to tear apart the last vestiges of our being? Do we build neither a wall to block love from coming in nor a bridge to let hate come in, but a scale to decide everything on a case by case basis? Does this allow us the critical thought to decide what love and hate is, and how it collectively plays out? We've all had traumatic and broken hearted experiences that make us wonder if we'll ever find what we're looking for. Once we define what love and hate mean to us, we'll know what to hang on to and what to get rid of. We'll see by consciously pursuing this balance, walls will be erected to keep out darkness, and bridges to usher in light. Our world and our nation is entering a new time where we'll collectively ask what we stand for. Everything is so blatant because we ignored it for so long, making us unable to hide. If we still choose to ignore, we're no longer hiding, we're complicit. Positive change isn't made with neutrality, but action. Do we want to control our actions, or others?" ☺

FROM THE MIND OF CRITIC

JANUARY 19TH 2017

From the mind of critic: "If we're afraid of putting ourselves out there, are we afraid to let our voices be heard? Do we believe there are people much more educated, knowledgeable, and experienced whose voices are the very foundation of the ether, so why would anybody listen to us? Do we believe our voices matter? Are we so concerned with our message having a positive effect, that we spend our time looking for the right in, instead of taking advantage of opportunities, however small their windows might be? None of us like being judged, honed down, and put inside a box. However, It's not the act of being judged that guides our future, but how we react. If we're afraid of what somebody might say or think, we might think inside a bubble is the safest place. Sometimes this fear is a bigger roadblock to our progress, than all judgmental people combined. Once we realize standing up and speaking out is scary, but freeing at the same time because we're being honest with ourselves, we'll see there's a reason that "we have nothing to fear but fear itself" is an old cliché. Putting ourselves out there might end in failure, but if we never put ourselves out there, success will never be a possibility. What do we have to lose besides our self-imposed roadblocks?" ☺

FROM THE MIND OF CRITIC
JANUARY 20TH 2017

From the mind of critic: "Whether we want to say happy inauguration day or happy GDMF day, how can we unite? Whether we want to completely blow up the system, or make the system work better for all of us, how can we unite? When some of us don't take the new president seriously most of the time, but cheer him other times, while some of us know he has no elected or military experience, hence no public record to analyze, hence we take his words and previous actions seriously because there is nothing else to analyze, how can we unite? When some of us whole heartedly support the new president because we agree with what he's trying to pull, because we ourselves have been stripped to our core, so we think everybody who looks or thinks different is out to get us, while some of us know what he's trying to pull is nothing new but has never been this overt, so we fight tooth and nail against it, how can we unite? Something very few of us saw happening, is happening, today, January 20th, 2017. There's a huge collective "how did we get here" air floating around. I'm not going to list all the reasons we should have seen this coming, all the issues we never fully dealt with and continued to kick down the road for generations, would take a volume of books.

However, once we realize that we're being controlled by the elite through the few crumbs they allow us to have, which cause us to divide into racial, religious and ethnic tribes, we'll see we're the same people with the same issues. We can unite, when we realize we're all in the same boat" ☺

FROM THE MIND OF CRITIC JANUARY 21ST 2017

From the mind of critic: "If we long for yesterday, because we believe times were so much better, do we long for tomorrow for the same reason? Are we so upset, angry and hurt about how bad things currently are, that we want to turn back the clock to a time when we think those things didn't exist? Is the anger we feel right now so strong, that we see wanting to turn back the clock as why we're at this moment? Is the only rational thought we have not how much worse are things going to get, but how much better are we going to make things because we're all awake? If we're screwed, doomed and there's no hope for the future, why should we even pay attention? We should just turn off, and tune out. This may be the feeling of many as we embark on the presidency of a man, which just thinking of him as president, makes me vomit in my mouth. What prevents me from doing so is not an iron stomach, but knowing the world of our dreams, a country that represents all people, is within our grasp. You might ask, how can that be when extremists will destroy all safety nets, environmental regulations and half the government itself, so they can give more money to the top 1/10th of 1%? I see a brighter future in all that, because it's a chance to put down for good all the darkness done behind closed doors, now being done in the open. This is a collective opportunity to make our lives better, and squash negativity.

If we tune out more than before, we're playing right into their hands. Their plans will go into maximum overdrive, because they want us to tune out, and not pay attention to what they're doing. We mustn't long for yesterday or for tomorrow, we must long for today. If we take action to better us all, giving up won't be an option." ☺

FROM THE MIND OF CRITIC
JANUARY 24TH 2017

From the mind of critic: "If we live in an age of alternative facts, is it possible to ever win an argument? If the press is labeled as fake news whenever they cover something the president doesn't approve of, or are quick to point out his lies, is a free society still possible? Can we still claim to be a free society, when the only time the press isn't shunned, is when they agree with the president, and back up his "alternative facts?" Will we devolve further into a tribal society, because our thinned skinned president is compelled to respond to every slight, and to generalize every non-white population, because one member is seen as representative of an entire group? There's a reason the freedom of the press is not only enshrined in the constitution, but in the very first amendment. It's the duty of the press to be vigilant and courageous in holding those in power responsible. Our democracy only exists because we don't take our elected officials at face value, let alone the president's. Right and left wing dictatorships, along with communist, socialist and nationalistic regimes only function, because they have complete control over the media and messaging, thoroughly going through every bit to ensure nothing gets disseminated that makes the leader look bad. Many of us wanted the system shaken up with this election. However, whatever side we're on, I think we could all agree our country and our system should be more democratic, not less.

Arguing, compromising, negotiating or even talking to somebody who believes "alternative facts" are a thing, is like talking to a brick wall. The only thing that will get through is a jackhammer. We must be that jackhammer of truth." ☺

FROM THE MIND OF CRITIC
JANUARY 25TH 2017

From the mind of critic: "If we believe so much in a country that we pledge allegiance to a symbol of it, do we truly understand we can only remain a free country if we're indivisible, where all of us have equal access to liberty and justice? Do we believe liberty and justice are simply words we've been saying so long, that we don't think about what they mean, kind of like church on Sunday? Do we realize they're more than mere words we aloofly recite because of tradition, but are calls to action against anybody and anything that portrays themselves one way, while living completely differently? Words and language are something that matter, and don't matter at the same time. On one hand they help us make sense of the chaos, so we can faithfully, reasonably and realistically state our ideas so not only do we understand them, but so does the public. On the other hand, words can also greatly increase the chaos, making it a concept nobody can deny. This is done by distracting thinking and non-thinking minds alike, into believing things are true, without taking the time to figuring out if they actually are. What is the answer, how do we figure out what's true and what's not? First, we must ascertain what we think and believe, not what somebody else has told us to think and believe. Second, we must analyze the messages we receive past and present, and see if they're backed up with action. Empty words and promises are just that, empty.

We could promise all day that we believe in liberty and justice for all, but then heavily skew all advantages to one side. Trust but verify are words to live by, the more we verify the meanings of the words we hear and use, the more faith we have in them. Concepts and motives can never die, they can only be fogged over; may we all be fog lights." ☺

FROM THE MIND OF CRITIC JANUARY 26TH 2017

From the mind of critic: "If we want to play a sport because we're knowledgeable about it, and it brings us joy, but we're picked last or not picked at all, does it discourage us from playing? Does it make this team sport, this joint effort that's only equal to the sum of its parts, not actually a joint effort at all? Is it a series of small cliques that get along with other cliques, but not if somebody is an outsider, twisting in the wind because nobody wants to include them? The world, the country, the community we live in can be a scary and intimidating place. Which is why getting involved in our community and trying to make it better, can make us feel like we have a place, a voice and that we do matter. What's troubling is when we get involved in making our community better, but come to realize because we don't have a family, kids, own a business or a home, or are part of another community organization, we're the outsider amongst people who claim to be inclusive. Movements, organizations and community groups have always had disagreements about action and level of militancy. We might feel like an outsider, where others listen and then do whatever they were going to do anyway. It can't stop us. We must keep getting involved, standing up and demanding our voices be heard. We might be outsiders, but it's the outsiders who show the insiders they aren't who they claim to be." ☺

FROM THE MIND OF CRITIC JANUARY 27TH 2017

From the mind of critic: "If we don't walk the walk, if we're for something before we were against it, against it before we were for it, or supremely against a certain concept if our opponent supports it, but are stalwart supporters of that same concept if used by our person, are we hypocrites? If many of the things we say we're for are enacted by our opponent, do we really want to make positive change if we come out vehemently opposed? Are we only interested in improving our image, if it puts us one step ahead of the person next to us? Authenticity and quality of character have always been important factors amongst elected officials, but exponentially now. We're entering a collective turning point in our evolution as a country and a species, where we can go one way or the other. I'm not referring to left vs. right, which is a drama the media has made bigger, while simultaneously exposing its flaws and furthering conversation. The real battle is us versus them. The us, is people without political power and influence vs. the people who do. Using the power of the pen to further our needs over the needs of others, is the ultimate goal of those in power. They use the power of their office and of business accordingly. If we're against a president using too many executive orders that's fine, but we must be against it across the board. We can't claim it's perfectly fine for one president, and not for another. If we do, we are part of the problem because our word is shit.

We can either be trustworthy or hypocritical, we can't be both, and neither can our country or political system. Walking the walk means authentic action, not fake rhetoric." ☺

FROM THE MIND OF CRITIC JANUARY 28TH 2017

From the mind of critic: "If we know Hitler said, "when people hear a lie long enough they begin to believe it", do we truly understand "America first"? Do we believe it means putting our needs above others, and taking care of OUR people like never before? Do we realize the racist history of the term? Do we know it has been used to turn away families and children, who only wanted some semblance of a normal life? Do we know those human beings get sent back to the war, violence and persecution they escaped, only to be killed because the country that's supposed to be the beacon for liberty, humanity and hope, is the opposite? We're a nation of immigrants. We aren't a white Christian nation like our current leaders would like us to believe. They'd have us think that all people who come here because of the beacon of hope we represent, want to tear everything down. They don't want us to realize that those refugees, are exactly what makes America, America. Our current leaders also don't recognize they aren't federally recognized tribal members, so they too are immigrants. When white nationalists and the most disgusting form of bigotry infests decision makers at the highest levels, banning whole groups of people is how the purge starts. It's how Hitler began. The fact that yesterday, 1/27 was holocaust remembrance day, and also the day refugees were banned, should be burned into our brains because we've done it before.

German Jewish refugees, men, women and children were refused entry during world war 2, only to be sent back to die in concentration camps, all under a policy of "America first." The St. Louis manifest, look it up, it's true. We're cruising toward the violent, racist and fascist dictatorship we were specifically designed to stop. Will we stand up and put a stop to it, or will we become "good Germans" and turn a blind eye by believing lies. It's our choice, it's our future." ☺

FROM THE MIND OF CRITIC JANUARY 31ST 2017

From the mind of critic: "Is giving preferential treatment to Christians while barring Muslims, a religious test? If it's not a religious test but pits one religion against another, is it a terrorist recruiting tool? If this isn't a terrorist recruiting tool, does it stop the last 15 years of terrorists from arriving, because our current 18-24 month process isn't strict enough? Do we believe terrorists meant to do us harm would go through that process, considering how long they'd be in the public eye? If we believe all that, are we living in an alternate reality? Do we believe these things are true, even if they aren't backed up by evidence? If facts don't exist, maybe evidence, a free press and democracy don't either? Did some of us vote for this tin pot dictator in training because we believe in the radical, conspiratorial and racist ideology of his white supremacist top advisor? Did we vote for him because we never actually thought he'd do this stuff? Do we never believe what a politician says, and vote based on anything but the issues? Saying we're in some crazy times, is an understatement. We're in the early stages of a fascist dictatorship, which starts with ejecting immigrants. Do we restrict entry whether people are citizens or not, all under the guise of keeping us safe from people who want to take our stuff? We've seen many positive strides in the last few decades, but need to make many, many more. All the positivity we've gained is now being undermined.

If we still want to live in America, where people are truly judged by the content of their character, and not by what they look like, what they believe or where they come from, we must get off our ass and stand up. We must demand our rights, or they WILL be taken away. We must remember WHY freedom is NEVER free." ☺

FROM THE MIND OF CRITIC FEBRUARY 1ST 2017

From the mind of critic: "If we don't control our emotions when directing them toward public officials and world affairs, do we forget what's happening in front of our faces? If this includes evidence which backs up the very argument we're trying to make, do we act the same in our personal lives? If we're questioned about what we said or did, do we think it's a slight and immediately raise our voice and defensively angry up our tone because we feel threatened? Do we see questions as just that, questions, a want to know information one does not have, and therefore aren't threatened when somebody doesn't agree with us? Politics loom so large with so much happening, it's hard to know what's real, what's fake and what to think. The same can happen in our personal lives, when change arrives too fast, too much, or not at all. To not alienate the people close to us, we must ask ourselves constantly whether we feel threatened, lied to or challenged. If we do, we must tell the people we care about how we feel in a way, that isn't threatening or challenging. We might have the realization that even if we raise our voice, tone and body language in defense, it has the opposite effect. Rational thoughts and ideas can't be shared when we're all riled up, because heightened emotions, anger, tone and body language aren't based on logic and facts, but feelings. We all want to matter, and we all want to be heard.

We must not lose our thoughts in the fog of emotion, but strengthen them within the love we have for each other. Whether political or personal, honesty can be scary, but it is the light at the end of the tunnel." ☺

FROM THE MIND OF CRITIC FEBRUARY 2ND 2017

From the mind of critic: "If we as a country have chosen or been forced to swallow the red pill that sent us down the rabbit hole in the last election, are we surprised at the rabbit hole's breadth and depth? Do we believe we've contributed to its size, turning a blind eye with our inaction and neutrality for so long, that we can no longer sweep problems under the rug? Do we believe the rabbit hole was designed, built and maintained without our knowledge, and has nothing to do with our day to day lives? Any of us that have paid attention for any length of time, know that the bold, radical, evil and fascist acts now being undertaken, have always been done. The difference now is that the people currently in power are doing everything out in the open. Maybe we've contributed to this outpouring of overtness, by knowing these things have been happening, but haven't done anything to stop them. Maybe we didn't know it was happening, because we've internalized ignorance and blind loyalty which officeholders have beat into our heads. Maybe if we involved ourselves sooner, we could've prevented the rabbit hole from metastasizing into a terminal illness. It's helpful to look at history, to see where we may have gone wrong, and what lessons we can glean that we've yet to learn. What isn't helpful is looking back and wishing we could turn back the clock, to a time when everything was simpler.

This was also a time when we were more blinded to reality, a time that might have been good for us, but not others. When we realize the past is helpful for gleaning lessons but not for living, we'll see the more we concentrate on the here and now, the more we can brighten our future. If we created the rabbit hole, we can also cause its destruction. Once it's gone, which one could argue has already been done given our current overtness; we can act, or be silent. In the coming years, we might be completely destroyed, or create something more beautiful than our wildest dreams. Do we want to continue wearing our current frown, or do we want to turn that frown upside down?" ☺

FROM THE MIND OF CRITIC FEBRURARY 3RD 2017

From the mind of critic: "If we're all hypocrites by virtue of being human, because none of us live completely by our principles, how do we know what's real and what's fake? If the competing microcosms of our personal lives are filled with raw data we're attempting to analyze, how do we know what to take seriously, and what to shrug off? Since we get bombarded with messages, stories and news 24 hours a day, do we pick through all the crap to find the nuggets of humanity? Do we know crap flows out of the mouth of politicians and presidents requiring us to be vigilant, specifically so we can pick through the crap? Is this like picking a needle out of a 1000 acre field of haystacks? Does this cause us to move toward those who appeal to our emotions? Do politicians act like they know what they're talking about, just like we do? Do politicians know what they're talking about, and use it to disguise what they really think, just like we do? All skirmishes amongst politicians in Washington only happen, because of our skirmishes amongst each other. All sides see their treatment as unfair, and want action taken yesterday. We all create our own reality, by using people and experiences to decide what's true. This truth is our truth, not the truth. Facts are the macrocosm of all our individual truth microcosms. To identify the facts and not just our truth, we have to take in everybody's experiences, not just our own." ☺

FROM THE MIND OF CRITIC FEBRUARY 4TH 2017

From the mind of critic: "If life is simple and hard at the same time, is it because positive and evolutionary concepts take a while to sink into our life experience? Are some things easier said than done, because speaking involves words flowing out of our mouths, that we may or may not believe, and doing involves action which puts learned skills and overlooked variables on full display? Is it all just an amalgamation of saying and doing that has no rhyme or reason, only human nature that moves whichever way the wind blows? There are certain things amongst our daily routines and interactions that are new and world changing. Many things happen that we can't explain, don't want to explain, don't know or don't care about, which affect us all in different ways. This may cause us to learn a new subject or concept, so we can better explain to others and to ourselves what something is, and how it affects us. The learning process is never a bad thing, as knowledge always has and always will be the only power which truly enlightens. However, we do ourselves a disservice when we learn without experiencing. We might spend all day reading about something and how it affects others, making us think we know everything, which shuts off our learning process. This can set us back in our personal evolution because we don't truly know, feel and physically understand a concept. We can go back and experience what we learned, it just requires more effort.

Maybe the difference between simple and hard things in life is our conscious effort. Maybe life gets easier when we use our words to create action." ☺

FROM THE MIND OF CRITIC FEBRUARY 7TH 2017

From the mind of critic: "If we let fear justify a means to our end, are we selling out everything good and hopeful our soul used to contain? Do we know what we stand for and what we want? Are we scared into doing things which have a devolving effect, because we might have success in fulfilling our agenda? Do we cower in the corner because of somebody who sounds like they know what they're talking about? Can we pull ourselves out of this corner because these people only sound like they know what they're talking about, because we don't know what we're talking about? Whether we're a single parent trying to support our kids, a two income family barely scraping by, a successful professional, single, married, belong to any religion or culture, or an elected member of the House or Senate, fear should never dictate our actions. If we're scared of standing up for what we believe, because of the unrelenting backlash from those more powerful and influential, maybe we don't truly believe in our principles. Maybe we don't deserve our position. Maybe we know how important it is to the world to put our thoughts and ideas into the ether, but don't because we're worried how it'll personally affect us and our career trajectory. Are we such wussy babies that we don't deserve to be in the position we're in, other than being voted in by people who are bigger wussy babies than us? Listen, we're all human, and we need to stand up for ourselves, because nobody will for us.

Do we want to be wussy babies, and let the great American experiment be destroyed because we were to chicken-shit to do anything? Do we want to stand up and fight for what it actually means to be American? Are we for destruction or creation, it's that simple." ☺

FROM THE MIND OF CRITIC FEBRUARY 8TH 2017

From the mind of critic: "Are we supposed to look forward and not backward? If we want to change our neighborhood, community, town, city, county, state, country, world and planet for the better, how should we react if the powers that be are doing their damndest to turn back the clock? How are we supposed to move forward, if the old guard and the new recruits it controls are moving us back? Should we riot in the streets? Should we hold rallies and protests with an array of signs and megaphones? Should we storm political offices in person and on the phone, to make sure our congressman and senators know we're still here? Does it do any good if we all come to do our part, before we go back to our same old lives? Do senators and congressman see it as just the cost of doing business, knowing they just have to wait us out, before going back to what they were going to do anyway? There has been major uproar lately over the direction of the country. Some of us would argue that it was the same under Obama, but anybody who sees without the aide of rose colored glasses, knows this time is much different. We're seeing a bloodless coup take over every department of our American system, slowly turning us into an American version of the Soviet Union. Some of you might say I'm just some crazy liberal, who is overreacting about long held conservative beliefs.

Well if deleting multiple departments of government, taking away mandatory testing for new drugs, taking away public education, squashing dissent and a free press, where the goals are to jail or kill anybody who disagrees, then yeah, I guess I'm a crazy liberal. We must stop being blinded by fighting each other, and aim our attacks where they'd do the most damage; the gatekeepers and money changers who keep us fighting each other, so we won't fight them. We'll never see what's in front of us, if we keep glamorizing what's behind us." ☺

FROM THE MIND OF CRITIC FEBRUARY 9TH 2017

From the mind of critic: "If we're so divided as a nation that we think the other side is the epitome of evil, aren't our struggles basically the same? Does the whole concept of the other side and us vs. them keep us from ever uniting, because it fogs over the fact that we're not two sides of the same coin, but the same side of the same coin? Does this tribal separation represent a behavior as old as time itself, where we seek protection from those who look, speak, think and believe differently? Whether we describe what's going on right now as the greatest thing since sliced bread, the worst thing since Hitler or any of the million opinions in-between, we're all in the same boat. The bigotry, prejudice and downright hatred we feel, is fed by the moneychangers in the shadows who always have the final say. They use our division as a means of control, so they can do whatever their hearts desire. They know they'll win if we continue fighting each other. We'll lose if we stay ignorant to the brilliant scheme they're pulling. Have we ever asked ourselves why we keep fighting the same fights over and over, which get better before they get worse, and then better and then worse again, without ever truly getting better? All of us are hurting right now. We all see major changes and we're scared. We might feel like we have no control, and simply have to be happy with the bread and circuses we're tossed, while things get worse and worse at the top.

We must remember we're only helpless if we allow ourselves to be. The hate, ignorance and fear we feel, is exactly what's holding us back. Once we see why it's holding us back, we'll realize our rage has been miss-targeted. To move forward and evolve, we must make sure our enemies are actually the ones doing us harm." ☺

FROM THE MIND OF CRITIC
FEBRUARY 10TH 2017

From the mind of critic: "If fulfillment can be described as enjoying life's simple pleasures, does technology take it away? Does the inherently impersonal nature of social media make us forget what's in front of us, because all we see are images on a screen? Does the political vitriol, division and downright hatred both sides have for each other, make us forget how happy a walk on the beach or enjoying a sunset can make us? Are simple pleasures strengthened, because we need to take our minds off how bad things are, and how much worse they're going to get before they get better? Without accounting for our current political climate, there are many distractions and entities pulling us in a multitude of directions. This makes it hard to cling to anything, and may cause our minds to spin out of control. This is when simple pleasures not only strengthen our daily routines, but help us achieve our goals by freeing our minds from the propaganda fog. That way we see what we truly want, and discover ways to bring them into our lives. The difference between satisfaction and contentment is like the difference between happiness and joy. One is fleeting, while the other long lasting. One stops our progress. The other keeps us moving forward. The trick is figuring out which is which. The way we do that, is by enjoying life's simple pleasures. The way we do that, is by not letting any of the current bullshit get us down, but spur us to action. Who doesn't want action?" ☺

FROM THE MIND OF CRITIC FEBRUARY 11TH 2017

From the mind of critic: "Are we a fascist dictatorship, or a constitutionally protected democratic republic? Do we racially profile all non-whites based on generationally imbedded ignorance, or do we base our judgements on the content of character and whether people have committed an actual crime? Do we think a gun rights protest consisting of white people is okay, but a gun rights protest consisting of black people is something to fear? Do we harass, persecute, arrest, imprison and punish white people for crimes the same as black people? Are we a nation that shuns people for escaping poverty and violence to come here, because immigrants do us harm? Do we believe these people are taking our jobs and benefits while not paying taxes? Are we in such dire straits economically that we blame all the scary brown people for our plight? Do we blame the law abiding people who come here to work and make a better life for their family, or the employers that pay below a poverty wage with no benefits? Do we believe health care is a right or a privilege? Do we believe education is a right or a privilege? Do we believe terrorist acts are only committed by Muslims, or by anybody including white Christians because of religious and/or political ideology? Do we believe we're fighting terrorism or feeding it? Do we believe the president has ultimate authority and can't be challenged, or that laws still apply because powers are separated into three branches of government?

Do we believe there's a difference between Trump saying a president can't have conflicts of interest, and Nixon saying that when a president does something it isn't illegal? Do we believe a president should profit off of the office they hold, and promote their friends' businesses by giving them special favors to boost their bottom line? Do we believe liberty and justice for all is just part of a pledge we say but don't think about, like going to church? Do we believe in the power of words, and the great country we can be when we finally live out our creed like we never have before? These are questions we should be asking ourselves if we authentically believe in freedom. If we don't ask ourselves these things, are we feeding our inner hypocrite?" ☺

FROM THE MIND OF CRITIC FEBRUARY 14TH 2017

From the mind of critic: "If we pushed things to the limit when we were teenagers just to see what we could get away with, do some of us never grow out of that phase? Do we have a right to push things as far as they'll go under the law, so we can take advantage of every opportunity to better ourselves in ways not expressly spelled out as illegal? Is that the American way? Do we have a moral obligation as human beings on this floating blue orb we call earth, to not take advantage, step on or push down others? Do we act so we can have a little bit more if something isn't expressly illegal, but is unbecoming of anybody who considers themselves a good steward of our collective species? Is that the American way? It's not unusual to test limits when we we're young, specifically to discover what the world is all about. We were born without knowledge, and learn from our parents and/or other outside stimuli. Problems appear when we're older and should know better, but still provoke people by acting only to get a response. This can cause us trouble if we're a working class adult trying to scrape out a living, amongst others in the same boat. We take out our frustrations on each other, instead of the people on the top who actually deserve our ire. This concept of pushing limits till they break causes even more havoc if we're a CEO, or an elected office holder. We might feel like we're above the law, because laws are only for little people.

We push things to the limit in favor of progressive change, or in favor of regressive change; which brings us back to intent. Do we have to lift others up to get ahead, or push them down? If the road to hell is paved with good intentions, it's because the actions that follow push others down, instead of building them up, which makes the stated intentions false. When stated intentions are false, civilians as well as presidents will attempt anything their imagination can conjure. Their success depends on the amount of pushback they receive." ☺

FROM THE MIND OF CRITIC FEBRURARY 15TH 2017

From the mind of critic: "If we got to get out of this place if it's the last thing we ever do, do we have another destination in mind when the words pass over our lips? Are we so upset and disheartened with our current situation, that our desired destination is anywhere but here? Will this mentality drive us to places we didn't think of, because we're journeying into the unknown without preconceptions? Are we so desperate to get anywhere but here, that we're pulled in directions we know drag us down, because we haven't put any thought into where we'd like to end up? Whether it's a physical, emotional, political, philosophical, financial or spiritual place, we all need to change our direction periodically. Getting too comfortable makes us stagnant, and makes us think we know everything; when the only thing we're experts on is the contents of our bubble. This is when we can't simply talk about the bad things we want to destroy, but all the good things we want to build up. If we don't figure out our goals, hopes, dreams and the direction we want to go, somebody will push us in a direction that benefits them, while conveniently forgetting about us. This can make us feel cared for, because somebody is thinking for us. We allow it because of their pronouncement of having our best interests at heart. This is when they screw us over. Now, they might do the opposite, and push us to a place that's to our benefit, forcing us to get out of our own way.

However, unless we utilize the critical thought required to tell the difference, we're guaranteed to be dragged down, while we build up somebody else. Whether we're a resident or an elected office holder, those in illusory positions of power will always tell us what to do, no matter what station in life we're at. We can't borrow somebody else's shovel to dig ourselves out of a rutted hole, we must use our own." ☺

FROM THE MIND OF CRITIC FEBRUARY 16TH 2017

From the mind of critic: "Do the loud voices of the majority drown out the minority, only because they don't realize it's the minority? Does the soft voice of the minority get drowned out by the majority, only because it doesn't realize it's the majority? Does volume level in an argument depend on passion level? Many of us want to speak out on a number of issues these days. Everything is extremely raw, and more overt than it has been in a generation. Sometimes we don't stand up and speak out because we know we'll be drowned out, sometimes we just think that'll happen. Sometimes we build up the courage to speak out, only to be shouted down. We must remember more volume in an argument, doesn't always mean more knowledge. Sometimes we have to yell and scream and stomp our feet, to overcome the fact that we don't have any idea what we're talking about. Sometimes we're actually knowledgeable but are afraid to speak, because we don't have as much experience as those who are loud and obnoxious. They say the elites, gate keepers and moneychangers who have ruled governments and economies for millennia, have to beware the silent majority. The fact is, if that majority stays silent, those at the top have nothing to fear, as their loud voices will continue ruling the day. However, if that silent majority decides to become the vocal majority, and stands up loud and proud on a consistent basis, there's nothing gate keepers could do.

Being loud or silent doesn't denote what's right or wrong, but if we're afraid to stand up, we won't know the definition of either. Positive change isn't made by speaking loudly, but by speaking consistently." ☺

FROM THE MIND OF CRITIC
FEBRUARY 17TH 2017

From the mind of critic: "If we can't see the writing on the wall, are we listening to what people say is right in front of us, instead of actually seeing what's in front of us? Are we afraid to trust our instincts, because louder and more knowledgeable voices sound like they know what they're talking about? Have we never paid close attention because no friends or family ever showed us how? If we started being mindful now, would it seem like such a foreign concept that our world would flip upside down while making our head explode? Exploring, explaining and understanding new concepts can be hard, especially if we're a cynical adult whose beliefs have hardened from life experience. However, just because some things are different than anything we've ever done, doesn't mean they aren't worth it. We might surprise ourselves with what we can accomplish when we get out of our own way. There are many things, events and concepts useful to our tool kit, items we can pull out and use when life presents a challenge. None of these concepts are more important than deciphering and translating the writing on the wall. We must see how it can be applied in real time to our life, and a particular situation. We must pay attention to all messages, and realize they're the first step. Realizing a good portion of them are bullshit with minute bits of truth mixed in is the second step. Once we realize how these truth bits apply, we see how even bullshit plays an important role by showing what pulls us from the truth.

In the land of alternative facts, truth can be hard to find. Yet, if we see the buildup, we'll know what's coming, and will be able to stop what's detrimental. We must always pay attention to the writing on the wall no matter the author. It might reveal a truth we thought no longer existed. The clues are there, we must simply allow ourselves to see them." ☺

FROM THE MIND OF CRITIC FEBRUARY 18TH 2017

From the mind of critic: "If projection is an effective way for politician's to get their point across, how come we only agree when it's directed at somebody we dislike? Is it because we agree with negative messages directed at people we dislike, and only notice projection if it's directed at somebody we do like? Is it because we only stand up for language and free speech when we agree, and think its hate speech or devolving speech when we don't? When there's something we don't like about ourselves, we'll project onto others exactly what's wrong with us. We'll fail to admit our issues, and pass blame. Since politicians and their conniving talents are an outcropping of the way we treat each other, it's no wonder that when we reach positions of power, we anxiously degrade others. Fixing our politics means fixing ourselves. We must look inward to see what our personal issues actually are, and what we can do to fix them. We might feel like deflecting issues onto others, because it makes our issues temporarily disappear. The kicker is they return fiercer. We may push them away again, but they'll keep coming back until we deal. That said, projection isn't illegal and it shouldn't be as it falls under free speech. If all speech isn't protected than no speech is protected. We must realize projection exacerbates our problems. However if projection doesn't happen, we wouldn't be able to detail wrongs.

Our problems get worse the more power and influence we gain. If we want to stop continuously passing blame until the end of time, we must never be afraid to talk openly and honestly to each other. We must realize that everybody has the right to disagree with us, and we have a right to disagree with them. That concept is called conversing. If we had fruitful and non-judgmental conversations, not only would projection disappear, but so would animosity. We must never be afraid to wave at somebody and say hello, it could start the conversation which saves the world." ☺

FROM THE MIND OF CRITIC FEBRUARY 22ND 2017

From the mind of critic: "If we all sat through puppet shows when we were younger whether we liked them or not, did we understand what they portrayed? Did we view them as fun, with characters on adventures teaching us valuable life lessons? Was there a quick summary at the end about how the whole story was one big moral metaphor? Did we see these fun characters portraying a story, lessons and guidelines for a successful life for what it really was? Did we see somebody behind the scenes pulling the strings, while telling a story that says one thing, but is actually a distraction? Were these shows controlled by somebody who thinks we can't see the strings they're pulling? We could make the argument that all of us have strings pulled by somebody. That all of us are pulled in directions we don't want to go, by forces we can't fully control. The concept of powerful people having their strings pulled by even more powerful people, playing out in song and dance to distract from what's actually happening, isn't new. The fact that the wool is being pulled over our eyes, and we're not doing anything when it's this blatant, is new. This concept has been brewing since we were young. By the time we're voting adults, we think it's just the way things are. Once we realize we're taught to not see the strings being pulled, but the singing dancing clowns in front of us, we'll see when elected officials including our current president engage in off the wall acts, they're disguising what they're really up to.

Puppet shows provide entertainment when we're younger and politics when we're older. As long as we never lose sight of the strings, we'll see how to cut them and make sure they never attach again. We need to stop being each other's puppets, and start being each other's counterparts." ☺

FROM THE MIND OF CRITIC FEBRUARY 23RD 2017

From the mind of critic: "If we feel like we're floating through life, are we unable to grip anything, while everybody else seems to be gripping tight? Do we feel our struggle is unique, and there must be something wrong with us because we're the only ones enduring? Do we know our struggle isn't unique, because nobody has a grip on everything, no matter how much they portray an image that they do? The Doors might have said "faces come out of the rain when you're strange", but Jim Morrison didn't take into account that we're all strange. When it rains, it falls on all of us. We're all part of the same struggle. We're all scratching and clawing to find our place. Some of us are at different stages of our journey, but we're all trying to get past the same obstacles. We're all trying to succeed because we want to be needed, and we want to matter. What keeps us down is thinking all other people know what they're talking about, because they're better than us, smarter and more successful. Once we realize that just because somebody is more successful or portraying they're smarter or more satisfied, doesn't mean they actually are, we'll see we're all floating through chaos. We're all trying to soak in as much good as we can, while making discoveries along the way. Will we all figure it out, maybe, we'll never know until we try.

We never need to feel alone because we're floating around, we need to feel part of the crowd specifically because we're floating around. We're all unique, and somehow we're all the same." ☺

FROM THE MIND OF CRITIC FEBRUARY 24TH 2017

From the mind of critic: "If a tree falls in the forest, does it make a sound? Does it make a thud so loud and thunderous, that it's heard around the world? Does the sound happen but have no effect, causing life to continue moving forward as if no sound was made at all? The old cliché of a tree falling in the woods is something we've heard a thousand times. Sounds happen all the time, whether we hear them or not. Sometimes we're enjoying the day, and are surprised by a sound we've never heard. Do we instantly feel uneasy because there could be many unknown sounds, which would flip our world upside down if we analyzed them for more than two seconds? Do we feel excited and eager specifically because there are unknowns out there? Will they drive us toward heights we never thought possible, because we went into the situation completely devoid of pre-conceived notions? While we can be startled and shocked by things we've never heard, we can also be motivated and driven. Granted if more people are around to hear something, more people will be shocked and/or motivated. The same fallacy that one person can't change the world, is the same as a tree falling in the woods. Both have sounds and effects, which are greatly affected by how many people hear them. The fallacy of these phrases is that the more people hear them, the more believe them. One lone person can't change the world, but many "one persons" can.

Just like if many trees fell at the same time, people would hear them everywhere. As we journey, there will be people who tell us we can't make change; that we could scream from the rooftops, and nobody would hear us. Singing loudly and proudly is not only our right, but our duty. We will be heard, as long as we don't allow anybody to shut us up." ☺

FROM THE MIND OF CRITIC FEBRUARY 25TH 2017

From the mind of critic: "If we're walking down the road minding our own business, and a bird shits on our shoulder, is it a sign of good luck for us, or the person laughing when it happens? Is it a positive sign because something that might have been a one in a million shot happened? Is it positive for the person who got the cheap laugh, because it's the funniest damn thing they've ever seen, allowing them to see something they never thought they'd see face to face? Is it positive for both the person shit on and the witness, because both were privy to an event that happens so rarely, it's proof there's a lot more to the world than meets the eye? The world is so big, chaotic, and filled with wonder, but at the same time it's small, ordered, and filled with routine. We can be grounded, yet still float around. Maybe we're trying to find the right balance, so we discover what's good, what's bad, what's real, what's fake, what will tear us down, and what will build us up. This makes finding balance infinitely more difficult, because what's good and builds us up, won't necessarily build somebody else up, and vice versa. The trial and error nature of life demands we live evolutionary experience as we learn it. If we learn it without experiencing it, we'll set ourselves back, and will have to work twice as hard to catch up. It makes us not want to put the work in because we have the knowledge, so why do we have to go through the motions?

This can cause us to feel lost, because we understand our actions before we take them, and are only able to sometimes stop them when they're detrimental. This can make us feel like we have no control and have no say, where we walk along amidst the chaos, fully aware its chaos. Then a bird comes along and shits on our shoulder. This makes us realize in no uncertain terms, we might be further ahead or behind in our journey, we might even be so open to it we feel every second, but there's always a big beautiful world out there. Good luck and positivity will find us and lift us up if we're open, but only when we realize how it affects everyone around us as well." ☺

FROM THE MIND OF CRITIC FEBRUARY 28TH 2017

From the mind of critic: "If the best things in life are free, are we assigning monetary value to something we can't fully describe? Do we need to know every detail of an item, so we can assess what ends up in the loss column, and which in the return column? Does a balance sheet need to be configured? Is assessing the value of an item, the same method as valuing an idea? What about an idea that doesn't correspond to anything physical? If money only exists because we put our faith in it, do ideas only exist because we put our faith in them? If we put faith in money and faith in ideas, does that assign a monetary value to ideas, whether we think about it or not? If we can't describe something is it free, or are we unable to describe the value? Love, peace, hate, ignorance, intolerance and joy are all concepts we can't fully describe. We can describe what they mean to us, but not what they mean for others, because it changes for everybody. None of us would admit hate, ignorance and intolerance are the best things in life, and most of us would admit that love, peace and joy are. Definitions of these ideas change from person to person. What's best for us might not be the best for somebody else. Life can be very chaotic, events happen that we can't explain. Our minds must have something to cling to, organizing universally chaotic ideas in a way that doesn't make us spin out of control.

So when we say the best things in life are free, we're simply putting subjective ideas in a form we understand. If we know those best things change from person to person, what are we really making less chaotic? For all of us to lead a fulfilling and satisfying life, we need to stop thinking in terms of free and not free, but in terms of building up and tearing down. It's the only barometer which truly matters." ☺

FROM THE MIND OF CRITIC MARCH 1ST 2017

From the mind of critic: "If a bird glides along with the breeze, letting itself be carried whichever direction the wind blows, does it's life become easier? Does a bird's life become less stressful and more enjoyable, because it doesn't have to expend physical energy to get anywhere, or mental energy to think of where to go, because another entity is so graciously expending it for them? Does a bird's life only appear more enjoyable because their thinking was outsourced to a puppet master, instead of the bird choosing its own direction by utilizing thoughts inherent to its survival? Critical thought and making our own decisions are not only what we were designed for, but how we grow and evolve. We must be vigilantly courageous to stay conscious of what's in front of us. If we allow ourselves to blow around in the wind, ceding control to whatever pushes us forward, ignorance will wash over us by emitting the aura of a stress-free life. The ones pulling the strings have a much more sinister motive. They want to pacify the public until they rebel, and put an end to not only the distractions, but everything the distractions were meant to cover up. Do we want to be the bird that glides without a care in the world? Do we want to be the bird that charts its own course, because we do care? Are bread and circuses all we're after, or are we after something more? Are we human?" ☺

FROM THE MIND OF CRITIC MARCH 2ND 2017

From the mind of critic: "If we're continuously surprised by how much worse things get, do we set the bar so low, that a knuckle dragging, mouth breather who can string coherent sentences together is seen as a success, simply because they aren't ranting and raving? Does a softer tone indicate a softening attitude toward other cultures and ethnicities, even if the concepts displayed stay the same? Is quintessential double-speak when someone speaks in humane tones, specifically so they can speak more inhumanely? Is this because most people listen to tone and not words? One concept recently introduced, is that we can't take the president literally. That sometimes his words don't represent how he actually feels. That sometimes he gets caught up in the heat of the moment, and appeals to people's emotions, because he believes that's what people want to hear. There are leaders in the past who have appealed to emotions, leaders who warned about the incoming scourge of immigrants, who will take our jobs, our women and our way of life. Leaders who even went so far as to endorse registries for those immigrants, for people to add to whenever they felt the need to rat on their neighbor because they didn't like them. These leaders were called dictators, stamping out dissent by calling all negative news fake. They murdered, disappeared and discredited opponents.

They built up nationalistic fervor by stating the reason for all problems, were the dirty foreigners flooding in. If things are so bad we think we need a dictator to muscle the American experiment into the 21st century, we're simply being lazy and ignorant. In the coming days, weeks and years we can either fight back, or sit idly by. Do we want to forever celebrate mediocrity, or sustainable and long-lasting positive change?" ☺

FROM THE MIND OF CRITIC MARCH 3RD 2017

From the mind of critic: "If the highway of life is jammed with broken heroes on a last chance power drive, is it the person that believes they're broken, or the society? Is it society that deems them a hero, or themselves? Who pray tell determines that the last chance is really the last chance, which gauges how much power is needed? Are our personal struggles, part of the bigger struggle? Do we think believing differently divides us, but actually proves we're on the same side of the same collective coin? Ultimately we determine our destiny, with varying degrees of influence from the outside world depending on our family, history, environment, culture, ethnicity or time period lived. While being a hero consists of a deed or an event that involves the outside world, it is us who decides whether the challenges and adversity we face breaks us. We determine whether it's our last chance, by deciding to either give up when we have no energy left, or to use every ounce of power we feel in our bones. Once we realize the struggle we endure makes us think it's only happening to us, but is really happening to everyone, we'll see that it's never our last chance, and we're never broken until we say we are. The highway of life is jammed, but only because we're all searching for joy, fulfillment and truth simultaneously." ☺

FROM THE MIND OF CRITIC MARCH 4TH 2017

From the mind of critic: "Are the reasons we can't unite as numerous as the reasons we can? Do these excuses prevent us from taking action? Do we understand reasons for division because they're fewer, and have been baked in for generations? Do we view unifying reasons as understandable, but we're intimidated because their numbers reach infinite proportions? Does this make it difficult to choose, causing an overwhelming sense of hopelessness to be chiseled over generations? Do we feel the notion of "it is what it is" is a false narrative, because some of us who have seen injustice and atrocities, have risen up and made positive change, flipping around the way things are? Excuses are like assholes, just like politicians are like diapers. They're not only full of shit, but they explode all over people around them, infecting every living soul if they go unchecked. We must constantly ask why we feel the way we do, and whether we're purposefully stopping progress because it seems terrifying. The fact is new, unknown and unfamiliar concepts are scary. However, we must also ask why they're scary, and would we rather do the same old thing even though we know it's detrimental. Once we realize the reasons we can unite vastly outnumber the reasons we can't, we'll see we can come together around most things, we just have to be open. We need to stop being our own worst enemy, and start being our own biggest cheerleader." ☺

FROM THE MIND OF CRITIC MARCH 7TH 2017

From the mind of critic: "If security fear rises so high, we think giving up freedoms is worth the illusion of safety, do we deserve to be safe? Do we believe the only way we'll feel safe, is if somebody else isn't? Do we approve of losing inherent American freedoms, if they're only taken from those viewed as a threat? Do we think all of us can only be safe, when we're all safe? Do we think this only happens when we respect each other enough, to treat each other like we'd like to be treated? Do we rail against the government controlling what we do or believe, but not against things we don't? Do we believe we're an island? After 200 years and war after war, after incoming immigrant group after incoming immigrant group, we're still America and we still exist. We still exist as the greatest experiment of melding different cultures and people into an amalgamation of humanity, because everybody is supposed to get a fair shake. The argument we've never fully lived up to our ideals is a fair one. However, every time a group of immigrants is generalized, a minority group marginalized and humanity exorcised, the moral arc of the universe bends toward justice. Once we realize none of us are safe until we're all safe, we'll see taking away somebody's dignity and human rights for the illusion of security, puts us all in danger. The true measure of a society is how we treat the least among us, not the paycheck writing elite." ☺

FROM THE MIND OF CRITIC MARCH 8TH 2017

From the mind of critic: "Is there a month for Black history, Women's history, Latino history and for other marginalized groups, because we've treated them so bad the rest of the year? Are we trying to give them representation? Do we think if they get a month, we don't have to think about them the other 11? Is it part of a long history of token responses, where instead of dealing with an issue in its entirety, we do the bare minimum, and kick the can down the road when the issue blows up in our face? Taxation without representation has been a concern since before the Declaration of Independence. Hell, it was one of the main reasons we left England in the first place. When people don't feel they're represented truthfully, they either roll over or fight back. Recognizing this, the powers that be offer small responses which take minimal effort. Making them look good even though they could care less, because they understand the political advantages gained from satiating the public. While that satiation isn't close to good enough, and can be detrimental if it's the only action taken, it can still be seen as going too far. The cries for a white history month and of reverse racism are decried by those who don't realize every month is white history month. Reverse racism is a concept thought up by people who think they couldn't possibly be racist because they have black friends.

If we treated each other like human beings all year, we wouldn't need monthly celebrations, because the entirety of our history would be taught, warts and all. We can stamp out racism with humanity every time we wave at a stranger, simply because both of us are human. Token responses eject from our toolkit, once "one and done" is no longer a phrase we live by." ☺

FROM THE MIND OF CRITIC MARCH 9TH 2017

From the mind of critic: "Is anger necessary to rouse passions, imploring us to take action? Does denying what's in front of us make us angry, because we could've taken action sooner? Does seeing the unfiltered truth, and understanding the schemes and under-handed relationships committed under our name make us angry? Can we move past anger by not being fearful of the unknown, but by excitedly diving in head first because of all the amazing possibilities? Anger, like other emotions features a good and bad side. Anger can be good if it spurs us toward thoughtful action, once we slow down enough to think. These clear thoughts are never achievable when we're angry, because we're running on emotion. We can't stop emotions, but we can control them by not making decisions when we can't think straight. A lot of events and issues make us angry these days, no matter what end of the political spectrum we find ourselves on. Once we focus anger on our true target, we'll see useful action means thinking honestly and clearly so our action makes a difference; instead of adding fuel to the fire that has been burning for thousands of years. If we're grieving a death, anger might emit when we stop denying what's in front of us. However, if we fully accept what's in front of us before we get angry, we won't completely fly off the handle.

If we keep fighting each other forever we'll live within our anger, giving us the false picture we're thriving. To make positive change through thoughtful action, we must be thoughtful to each other." ☺

FROM THE MIND OF CRITIC
MARCH 10TH 2017

From the mind of critic: "If speaking truth to power prevents our constitutional democratic republic from going the way of the Roman Empire, then how come those in power are so afraid of truth being spoken? Is power afraid truth will uncover its methods of greasing the wheels, and cause the system to fail? Is power afraid of truth not because they're afraid the system will fail, but because they're afraid they'll personally lose power? Many similarities have been proven over the years comparing our empire, to the Roman Empire. We both had military bases all over the world, as well as political, financial and economic centers to foment control. That massive power can only exist if truth is painted as the enemy of the state, but only if that truth didn't come from power. Power is okay with truth if it's their truth. If somebody else's truth confronts theirs, it's automatically false and a lie. Can our American system survive when the people's truth is spoken? Will the system better represent the people, if power isn't concentrated into hands too inhuman to understand it? Can truthful power be held, or even exist? Is truthful power an oxymoron? If we want to live the life we see in front of our face and feel in our hearts, and not what some power broker tells us through our ears, then speaking truth to power is imperative. We have nothing to lose, and only positive and collective consciousness to gain." ☺

FROM THE MIND OF CRITIC
MARCH 11TH 2017

From the mind of critic: "If love conquers all, what the hell is it waiting for? Is love an all-knowing omnipotent power, which cherishes its enemies, and smites its enemies? Is love a separate entity from us, coming in and out of our lives without our say so, and sometimes without our knowledge? Do we as humans have a completely symbiotic relationship with love, where we don't exist if it doesn't exist, and vice versa? Many indescribable and completely subjective concepts exist in the ether of our psyche, not least among them hate, sadness, money, credit, jealousy, joy, happiness and of course love. These concepts only exist because we put our faith in them. If we didn't think they were real, they would cease to be. If we create our own realities, and put our faith in certain concepts that make up those realities, will hate and darkness disappear if we stop putting our faith in its existence? Will love and joy also disappear if we stop feeding them, because we expect them to fall out of the sky and into our laps? We must believe in love for it to appear and absorb into our soul. If we believe love is impossible for us, we'll be brought right to the cusp, believing it might actually be possible, only to see it pass us over again and again. This can make us cynical, which repels love even more; because deep down we didn't think it was possible anyway, and are simply being proven right.

Once we believe love is possible and we're deserving of it, we'll picture it playing out. This is when love washes over us like rain. Love does conquer all, but we're the conquerors, and love is the weapon." ☺

FROM THE MIND OF CRITIC MARCH 14TH 2017

From the mind of critic: "If hell hath no fury like a woman's scorn, what about a man's scorn? What about a sister's, brother's, mother's, father's, son's, daughter's, uncle's, aunt's, nephew's, niece's, friends, or lover's scorn? What about an immigrant's scorn, a senator's, congressman's, activist's, Christian's, Muslim's, Jew's, union member's or artist's scorn? What about a president's scorn, does hell hath no fury like a schoolyard bully and narcissistic con-artist, when he's behind the bully pulpit? No matter our gender, family, sexual orientation, religion, ethnicity, culture or station in life, we all get mad. No matter our label, some of us get madder than others and some less, because we're all human. No group believes monolithically, no matter how deeply imbedded stereotypes are. All movements and groups have disagreements within them about action and level of militancy. Once we realize that generalizing a certain group, because we see them as different due to not having or wanting knowledge about them, we'll see the more information we gain by asking questions, the more we'll see disagreements in other's groups, are the same disagreements we have. This is how what makes us different, actually makes us the same. Hell does hath a lot of fury, but not nearly as much as us when we've been taken advantage of and been lied to repeatedly. Focusing our true collective fury, destroys the illusion of power." ☺

FROM THE MIND OF CRITIC MARCH 15TH 2017

From the mind of critic: "If we all reap what we sow, how come some reap more than others? Do we reap what others sow, riding coat tails until we swoop in and take credit for somebody else's hard work? Do we willingly and unwillingly allow others to do the swooping, not believing in ourselves enough to benefit from the fruits of our labor? Are we all trying to find success and love amidst a sea of chaos, taking advantage of every opportunity, no matter what cave it decides to crawl out of? We all want success, love and joy, and are willing to utilize various effort levels. Some of us are convinced that as long as we end up on top, it doesn't matter how many heads we step on along the way. Some of us are so practiced at self-sabotage, we can't picture success being our reality. When somebody else takes credit and praise due us, and changes the original intent of our hard work, it plays into our imbedded self-image of the person who always falls short. One issue that could fix this dilemma, which all sides could agree on, is accepting responsibility. If we think we can never do wrong and have never done wrong, we'll forever pass the blame. Not only will the buck never stop with us, we'll never reap the fruits of our hard work, unless we steal them from somebody else. If we want to reap what we sow we will, for all our actions. We can't choose either or, because we'll never know what each truly means.

If we can't be accountable to ourselves, how can we expect to be accountable to others, let alone 300 million Americans?" ☺

FROM THE MIND OF CRITIC MARCH 16TH 2017

From the mind of critic: "If the rain falls harder, faster and with more frequency, will it evaporate quickly enough to allow drying out periods? Are these drying out period's imperative, so we remember what normal life is like? Is drying out a pipe dream, because we're so waterlogged from all the rain that has fallen, and all that's to come? Life is and has always been a balance, a teeter totter of good and evil, positive and negative, yin and yang. We go through periods of fear and hate, hope and love and vice versa. This depends on who we have in power, and the prevailing consensus of the population. We can't completely stop these swings from happening, they occur naturally due to our environment and increasingly invasive human evolution. However, we can speed up, slow down, strengthen and weaken these cycles with our thoughts, feelings and actions. We must ask ourselves on a constant basis, what influence we have? We have enormous power to ease the destruction of humanity, and to stop the corporate fascist takeover of this country guised as regressive populism. We must see how this power affects us and others around us. Making things worse for others just so things will be a little better for us, doesn't make us safer, it gives the power structure more time to plan our demise. Their teeth are sunk in, and want to have fun playing with their food before they devour it.

We control our destiny as long we're honest about what's in front of our face. However, that honesty is only discovered if we take everything with a grain of salt, and don't ignore what we don't like; especially if it's a verifiable fact, and not the Orwellian double speak and think of alternative facts. We can make the rain fall harder, or we can make it lighten. It all depends on whether we decide to share our umbrella." ☺

FROM THE MIND OF CRITIC
MARCH 17TH 2017

From the mind of critic: "If painting is 90% prep work, do we refrain from painting at all because of all the work we have to do, before the work we have to do? Do we shy away from scraping, sanding and priming, because how is anybody going to tell when there's a fresh coat of paint? Do we not care what the paint looks like a few years from now, because having a fresh and shiny beautiful facade as fast as possible is all that matters? Would we rather have our hard work last for years to come, with paint not chipping or fading away, specifically because we spent long hard hours preparing? So many issues with so many facets with even more solutions evolve, mutate and completely change from person to person. This becomes tougher when we discover we have to lay a foundation, before we do the work we wanted to do in the first place. We can buckle down and hone in on what we want to accomplish, realizing more work is involved than expected, but isn't going to keep us from our goals. Do we completely turn off, go in guns blazing with no preparation, and fail miserably by instantly going down in flames? This not only wastes our time, but proves we didn't want to accomplish our goals as much as we thought. Do we want to accomplish great things? Do we expect them to fall in our lap? If we want to be a real painter and not just play one on TV, we must do the work required so the job is done right. If we do something half-ass, what's the point of doing it at all?" ☺

FROM THE MIND OF CRITIC MARCH 18TH 2017

From the mind of critic: "If the opposite of fascistic double speak is democratic truth defended by eternally courageous vigilance, why do we roll over due to the volume of blind faith we've consumed? Are we so tired from the consciousness we've espoused and expressed, that we stop critically thinking when listening or watching a point of view we agree with? Are we so anxious to succeed because of our enemies' defenses that we scour for any advantage, even if that means tuning out? Many of us actually pay attention, and ask questions. We care about other people and the world around us, no matter what side of the political, religious, philosophical or financial spectrum we find ourselves on. We all want to make a better world, but refuse on a constant basis to see the truth that will steadfastly unite us. Maybe we're scared of letting down our peers with opinions, that aren't as generationally imbedded as theirs. Maybe we have low self-esteem, and don't feel confident enough to stand up to the other side, let alone to our own. Maybe we aren't ready to have our world flipped upside down. Once we realize losing our humanity means losing our critical thinking, we'll see that taking care of the well-off better than the downtrodden will lead us to ruin, specifically because the grass is always greener on the other side; no matter what fertilizer we use.

If we want to get rid of waste and fraud, we must get rid of it on all levels, or we haven't gotten rid of any. Calling all truth seekers, are we willing to admit what has kept us at each other's throats, so we can unite and take on our true enemy? Are we ready to get over ourselves? ☺

FROM THE MIND OF CRITIC MARCH 23RD 2017

From the mind of critic: "If our clock stops out of the blue, whether it runs on batteries, electricity or solar, is a restart possible? Do we try and try and try to get our clock running again, getting angrier and angrier when we can't? As our rage boils over, do we understand why we're angry? Are we upset at the actual clock for stopping? Are we upset we took for granted that our clock was running, thinking it would run forever? Is it the clock we're mad at, or ourselves? Time is finite and infinite at the same time. If we expend effort to make our time enjoyable and productive, we can make moments last forever. It can also speed time up because we aren't focused on a physical number. The concept of time only exists because we have faith that it does. Like the proverbial pot of water that never boils when we stare, time will not run out either if it's the only thing we focus on. Of course who wants to spend all their time counting the physical essence of time, instead of enjoying each moment by fully immersing themselves? While enjoying each moment might make time seem like it's moving faster, it keeps moments flowing in and out in a continuous stream of uplifting energy. We can either hold on to time so hard the stream of life stops, or we can enjoy each moment for what it is, treasuring it while it's happening, then letting it end naturally. If our clock breaks, it's broken, that's it.

Do we want to spend our entire lives worrying about the day our clock will break, because it undoubtedly will? Do we want to spend our lives enjoying our time before our clock breaks? What will make our life worth living? What will make us smile?" ☺

FROM THE MIND OF CRITIC MARCH 24TH 2017

From the mind of critic: "If the streets are wet with pouring rain, do we adjust our driving speed accordingly? Do we slow down and put two hands on the wheel, but keep driving forward, realizing we can still get where we want to go even if it takes longer? Do we continue driving the same speed with one hand, because being relaxed is the best way to get where we want to go? Do we speed up, and swerve around people and cars as the rain falls harder, specifically because nothing is going to slow us down? Do we speed up because the rain isn't a roadblock, but motivation? The path we choose will always feature road blocks placed by us, and the outside world; as well as ruts, dips, and all sorts of baked in attitudes fueled by generations of uncritical thinkers. The way we drive is determined by our thoughts, feelings and actions, while those same thoughts, feelings and actions determine the road we choose. Once we realize moving forward is for our highest good, we'll see whatever speed we're traveling, the rain will try to run us off the road. It will make us swerve and spin until we forget what direction we're traveling. We may have to adjust our speed, but we're the only ones who can change our direction. We can slow down and have success, or we can speed up and possibly be run off the road. Adapting to our environment is how we evolve." ☺

FROM THE MIND OF CRITIC MARCH 25TH 2017

From the mind of critic: "If we're playing a board game whether we want to or not, do we roll dice to see how many squares to move forward? Are we scared to move at all, for fear our move won't turn out the way we wanted? Do we choose not to roll because although we won't move forward, we're guaranteed to not move backward? Do we roll the dice with fear, but since excitement overshadows that fear, we roll with gusto because although we may lose, we know we can't win if we don't play the game? Life is a game now and always has been, whether we admit it or not. This game involves risks that we can choose to take or not, with consequences that follow. We all have goals, hopes and dreams to make our life brighter. If we take risks by getting out of our comfort zone, and remind our soul we have the ability to surprise ourselves, we'll see until we step into the dark tunnel, specifically so we can reach the light on the other side, we'll be forever stuck in a hole with no way out. Life might be a game, but if we don't roll the dice, we'll never move forward." ☺

FROM THE MIND OF CRITIC MARCH 28TH 2017

From the mind of critic: "If we drive the same road to work every day, but then drive the same road on our day off, do we travel at the same speed? Do we drive with less urgency and more appreciation for our surroundings, when we're not racing to punch a clock? Do we drive with more urgency and less appreciation of our surroundings, when we are racing to punch a clock? Do we realize that we're traveling down the same road? So many of us fall into the same rut, organized by the same routine we follow day after day. Granted, life is basically chaos and we have to organize and explain it in a way that makes sense to us, or we'll be forever chasing the dragon. These routines allow us to go through life in a livable way. They also fog over our consciousness of the here and now. However, the best way to un-fog our consciousness is to never allow our routines to define who we are, just like we should never let our spontaneity define who we are. This is where balance helps, because it ensures we have both routine and spontaneity, and not more or less of one or the other. How does this play out? Instead of driving to work on the same road day after day, we can find a different route. Instead of going with the flow of the wind every time we're not working, we can plan what we want to do. When we get used to switching things up, we'll see we don't always have to switch physical activity, only our mindset.

We could do the same thing but look at it differently, or the same thing just on a different day. It's all about staying conscious of how we feel, how we're doing and what we're thinking. We could drive down the same road a million times, but if we slow down to look, and think about what's around us, the road will seem completely different. Life is all about journeying to discover joy, not about the destination of illusion. There might not be any there there, but having at least a rough outline of a destination, allows our journey to thrive. A balanced journey does a body good." ☺

FROM THE MIND OF CRITIC MARCH 29TH 2017

From the mind of critic: "If projection is how we win in politics, and consciousness is how we win in life, is it any wonder politicians tell us what we want to hear? Is our political system so messed up, that politicians hold one set of beliefs, but publicize a different set of beliefs for fear of being rejected? Is our real life so messed up, that we hold one set of beliefs, but display a different set for fear of being rejected? I had a political science teacher once tell me, that the way the system is structured, there's no way somebody could make it to a senior position without being crooked. Is it the same with life? Since our political system doesn't make us, but we make our political system, do we have to be crooked to succeed in life? Once we realize that being honest with our thoughts and feelings is how to get over generationally ingrained issues, we'll see projection disappear because it's only a means for covering up the truth. To fix our political system, we must fix our personal system. If we tell people what they need to hear instead of what they want to hear, or what we think they want to hear, we're proving a better system does exist. If we're trying to make our current system more authentic, we're halfway there. If we blame somebody for what we've done, we can't expect them not to blame us for what they've done. Responsibility, accountability and humanism will fix problems, as long as we start by looking in the mirror." ☺

FROM THE MIND OF CRITIC MARCH 30TH 2017

From the mind of critic: "If we believe flag burning should be illegal because it's a symbol of America, and burning a flag is like burning America itself, do we care more about the symbol than the country? Do we care about the aura of rights, dignity and liberty of all people more than the actual practice? Do we believe rights, dignity and liberty can only exist if it exists for all of us, especially the downtrodden and those with whom we disagree? Flag burning has long been a controversial issue, and will continue to be for the foreseeable future. We must ask ourselves if a symbol is more important than its meaning. Do we care more about the illusion of freedom then the practice? Do we want to feel safer, or do we actually want to be safer? There is a reason free speech is not only in the bill of rights as the first amendment, but also the first of part of that first amendment. Without free speech, our democracy, our democratic republic, our great American experiment would cease to exist. There is a reason dictators, despots, strongmen, warlords, fascists and oligarchs all want to give their people a symbol. The illusion of freedom makes the population believe they can stand up for what they believe in. The government will then give a token response that they're supporting the people, all while preventing major changes, further entrenching their power and influence through bread and circuses.

When free speech gets trampled, fascist dictatorship isn't far behind. Do we believe in America enough to know that without dissent and protest, we'd still be part of England? We might not believe that flag burning is an acceptable form of protest, but I'll believe dollars to doughnuts that we believe in dictatorships even less. Free speech never has and never will mean only things we agree with." ☺

FROM THE MIND OF CRITIC MARCH 31ST 2017

From the mind of critic: "If we take the same road day in and day out toward our intended destination, have we ever thought of a different road to get to the same intended destination? Do we think this different road will have unknown hazards and detours, meant to steer us 180 degrees from our intended destination? Do we think this different road is just that, different, and will lead to our intended destination simply from a different direction? Sometimes we see life as interconnected, and sometimes we see it as completely separate, all part of life's rich tapestry. Sometimes we see alternate routes but never take them, so we take the same old route because it's familiar. Sometimes we struggle with thinking we're the only soul on earth deciphering the decision making process. Sometimes we see ourselves and others struggling, but think our destinations are separate, which makes us further segregated and entrenched. Sometimes when we're truly connected we see our struggles as different, but realize we're all headed in the same basic direction, heading to that same basic place. We may all take different roads, but we're headed to the same basic place. As we find our unique paths, we can't borrow somebody else's. We can't downplay a path we don't agree with, because it degrades ours. Once we see we're all in this together, we'll realize none of us will get to that same basic place, unless we all do." ☺

FROM THE MIND OF CRITIC
APRIL 1ST 2017

From the mind of critic: "If we're all just bricks in the wall, who or what is the mortar that keeps us together? Are some of us "bricks " that make up the wall, while some us are "mortar" that holds it together? Do we make up the wall with the rich tapestries of our cultures, identities and experiences? Do we contain the mortar to hold the wall of life together, with some of us stickier than others? All humans have some level of detachment anxiety, as we pull ourselves away from and out of the wall, i.e. nature. The more we separate from the natural state we ALL come from, the angrier we become with ourselves and our situation. If we don't deal with this anger in a timely fashion, our attention will trend away from self-reflection, and toward others. We can become hostile, thinking the only reason we have problems, is because somebody else messed everything up. Once we get used to blaming others for our shortcomings, we'll start singling out those who don't look like us, don't believe like us, and are from some place we've never heard of. As the battle between our tribal group and their tribal group heats up, we become more and more blinded to the beauty of the natural world. We forget that all of us make up nature, and our collective inherent purpose is to take care of that nature.

Once we see not only how we make up the wall, but how the wall would fail if we didn't serve our purpose, we'll see how mortar is within all of us. Surprising ourselves doesn't have to be scary. It can be what saves us. We just have to get out of our own way." ☺

FROM THE MIND OF CRITIC
APRIL 4TH 2017

From the mind of critic: "If we couldn't reach the pedals on our first tricycle, did we give up ever riding a bike? Do we believe bikes were designed for other people to ride, so they could overcome challenges? Do we believe they weren't designed for us, relegating us to permanent serfdom, where the only challenges we overcome are what the bike designers allow? Do we believe that although these bikes were designed for others, it's not going to stop us from riding? Will we adjust and tweak the bike to fit our needs, because nobody is going to tell us what we can and cannot do? We all get discouraged when something doesn't work out like it's supposed to, or is made for somebody else entirely. Like how the grass is always greener on the other side of the fence. Once we realize our neighbors grass is always greener, we'll see ours can be green too with effort. We must ask ourselves do we care more about the amount of effort required, or the results. If we care more about the effort required, why do the results matter if we're locked into jealousy and trying to one up our neighbor? Our tricycle might not be designed for us, but the only way we can't ride, is if we refuse to tape blocks of wood to the pedals so we can reach them. We can ride, when we allow ourselves to move forward." ☺

FROM THE MIND OF CRITIC
APRIL 5TH 2017

From the mind of critic: "If we're against illegal immigration but love cheap labor, are we trying not only to possess the cake, but devour it as well? If we believe people are pouring over the border to take our jobs, are we willing to work for the same rate of pay? If we aren't willing to work for that same low rate with no benefits, if we don't want products to be expensive but aren't willing to ask why, if we want to state an opinion that's not based in fact, do we understand the consequential endgame protruding from our mouth hole? Do we treat each other as less human, so we can be treated as more human? Do we simply not have one critically thinking bone in our body? When we talk out of both sides of our mouth, we're still talking, just not thinking. We can't have cheap food without cheap labor. We can't have cheap labor without illegal immigrants. We can't have illegal immigrants if we didn't always want more. People come here to make a better life. We should be making that easier by shortening the citizenship process. People will try to do us harm that's true, but they come from every country around the world, not just the brown one to our south. If we love cheap labor but hate the illegal immigrants who provide that cheap labor, do we understand the magnitude of hypocrisy we're projecting? If we don't, maybe we should start treating ourselves like we treat others and see how far ahead we get." ☺

FROM THE MIND OF CRITIC
APRIL 6TH 2017

From the mind of critic: "If we have fog lights on our car, do they help us navigate through the fog? Do we appreciate any help that's provided, by bolting or strapping anything to our car, whether or not it works in practice? Are we skeptical of any help, because we've seen how hard it is to drive through fog with or without fog lights? Do we know the best way forward is not with some device that other people suggest, but instead moving forward at our own pace? Sometimes progress moves at a snail's pace, and sometimes a snail's pace would be like a top fuel dragster compared to how slow it goes. Progress can move quicker or slower depending on the thickness of the fog, but moving forward is always the goal. We might try waiting the fog out, hoping it dissipates enough to allow safe passage. However, the fog might condense and become worse, simply because of our inaction. Once we realize that fog lights only give us hope of moving through the fog, we'll see that hope without action devolves progress because of desperation. This doesn't mean something difficult isn't worth it, it just means it requires more effort. We can't only look for the easy way out, but for a way that works, period. People will give us advice all day long, but they're only suggestions, not orders. The only true orders come from our soul. We just have to make sure we're listening." ☺

FROM THE MIND OF CRITIC
APRIL 7TH 2017

From the mind of critic: "When we pull onto a busy freeway, do we adjust our speed accordingly, or do we go balls to the wall? Do we wedge into one of the many busy lanes, and then slow down so we're going with the flow of traffic? Do we continuously speed up and slow down as we weave through, because the flow of traffic will slow us down whether it's above the speed limit or not? Do we carve our own path by creating what we think is our place, vis-a-vie our purpose? These are questions we ask ourselves whether we're rich or poor, old or young, live in the city or the country, religious or non-believer, or are political or oblivious. Life is basically chaos, and we do our best to navigate. Many people try getting us to slow down or speed up, while attempting to squeeze us into a perfect little box they've designed. Once we realize it's not about fitting into our own box let alone somebody else's, we'll see there's no black and white answer to anything. It's not about only slowing, speeding, or staying, it's about doing all three at the same time. It's about fitting in, finding our place and making our way on the highway of life. This is how we find our purpose. We have to think to find, and find to be joyfully content. Isn't that life's true goal?" ☺

FROM THE MIND OF CRITIC
APRIL 8TH 2017

From the mind of critic: "If the rain is pouring with no end in sight, do we believe an umbrella will prevent us from getting wet? Do we think a giant umbrella will keep us bone dry, never to be affected by the rain no matter how hard it falls, specifically so we can ignore it? If this umbrella is brightly colored with flashy designs, that emit our personal disdain for precipitation, will it make the water bead off, allowing the speed of drying time to display how much more powerful we are than the rain? Do we say screw the umbrella and just walk through the rain with a good coat on, because we know the rain will never stop unless we allow it, no matter how torrential it becomes? To wear a raincoat or to not wear a raincoat, is like asking whether we should seek protection against free speech attacks and our way of life. Questioning whether or not to carry an umbrella, is like asking if we want every depersonalized aspect of our future to hit us all at once, obliterating the last remnant of our soul. Of course we need protection. We don't want to lose before the fight even begins. However, simply locating the right protection isn't going to stop the rain. It won't even slow it down. We must take it upon ourselves to move forward. When we let light engulf our soul, it spreads with every interaction.

Once we realize that light not only repels rain, but greatly lessens it, we'll see umbrellas and raincoats won't stop the rain, we do by undoing the illusion of its power through continuous conscious action. Who needs an umbrella or raincoat when we have our heart and soul?" ☺

FROM THE MIND OF CRITIC
APRIL 11TH 2017

From the mind of critic: "If a child says and does racist, sexist and homophobic things as they discover the world by testing limits, do we tell them they're wrong? Do we tell them that's not what we say to or about people? Do we enlighten them as to what's important? Do we tell them to judge people by what's on the inside, that if we don't have anything nice to say we shouldn't say it, and we should only treat somebody how we'd like to be treated? Do we ignore them or tell them they're not wrong, thereby instilling ignorance by leading through example, specifically because we judge by what's on the outside? Do we say mean and hurtful things whenever, why-ever and however we feel like it, because we feel more deserving of good treatment then others? Does this ignorance quickly and forcefully metastasize if not nipped in the bud at an early age? As we become adults, we all become like our parents whether we admit it or not. Their traits get instilled through constant communication, or deafening nonverbal naiveté. They follow us throughout life, and have an exponentially magnified effect if we hold public office. If we end up as President through election or otherwise, we're the epitome of what the people are, or what they ignore. If we don't like having a President who is a racist, sexist, homophobic, tiny handed baby man who bullies everybody in the schoolyard, we must ask whether we're racist, sexist, homophobic baby men ourselves.

Teaching kids the right way to be when they're young without ignoring them or their outbursts, would prevent somebody like President Donald Trump from even being a possibility." ☺

FROM THE MIND OF CRITIC
APRIL 12TH 2017

From the mind of critic: "If we're all drum majors for peace, justice, love and harmony, but dance to the beat of a different drum, do we ever run into the problem of too many cooks in the kitchen? If we're all courageously passionate about having our voices heard, do we drown other voices out because they're different from ours, and impede our voice from being heard? Do we allow other voices to be heard, specifically so our voice will be heard? Many times we fight and struggle so hard to be heard, that we forget other people are doing the same. We care so much about our rights and being treated fairly, that sometimes we see others fighting for their rights as our opponent. Sometimes we don't see others fighting for their rights as separate, but two sides of the same coin. Once we see human beings of all stripes always have and always will want to live free, we'll see fighting for our rights is a great thing, but when we see our fight as separate from somebody else's, ours quickly dissipates. We all came together to stop the Vietnam War. Then we splintered into separate groups, to fight for individual rights. Women's rights, youth rights, gay rights and others deserve to be fought for, but we stopped seeing how they were interconnected. If we're all drum majors for peace, love, justice and harmony we'll see fighting for rights, means fighting for ALL rights.

Once we see our collective success is symbiotic, we'll realize we might dance to the beat of a different drum, but we're all in the same band." ☺

FROM THE MIND OF CRITIC
APRIL 13TH 2017

From the mind of critic: "If we slow the pace of our daily activities to take care of ourselves, do we feel we're missing out? Whether we're sick, worn out, or simply need a break, do we feel bad for taking care of ourselves, because we're not attacking the million tasks in front of us, or the million tasks contained within us that haven't surfaced yet? Are we low simply because we're not feeling good? Does the fact that we're taking care of ourselves, remind us about the importance of healing quickly, so we can get back to accomplishing our goals and dreams? Not being productive when getting things done can make us feel bad. Just like being productive when not getting things done can make us feel overwhelmed. We need to eject from our comfort zone from time to time, specifically to remember we still have the ability to surprise ourselves. Sometimes we need to slow down and realize taking care of ourselves does make us less productive. It can also make our productive times more productive, by not trying to accomplish when our mind, heart and body aren't working together. Life is about finding what drives us, then finding our most productive time. Then doing what we can to be kind and take care of ourselves during those down times, which we all have and can't prevent. The difference between a temporary slowdown and one that's permanent depends on what's rolling around between our ears." ☺

FROM THE MIND OF CRITIC
APRIL 14TH 2017

From the mind of critic: "If life is all about discovering the cornucopia of unknown unknowns, what will life mean when we get answers? When things we don't know we don't know become things we do know we do know, does our purpose disappear? If we've defined ourselves as dissidents, rebelling against the powers that be, and then either the powers topple or we become the power, do we feel hopelessly lost because there's nothing to rebel against? Do we view this as the object of all our struggles, the finish line we've been working toward? Does it make us ready to take over, because it's exactly what we've been preparing for since we decided to stand up? Finding solutions to long imbedded problems has always been our goal. Where we mislead ourselves, is thinking we'll get to a place where we have all the answers. All we discover as we become more knowledgeable is more questions, kind of the opposite of the rebel. If we rebel against the power and then become the power, we'll find we can't rebel against the same things anymore. We'll have become the ones others rebel against. Once we realize life is rarely as it seems and objects are always closer than they appear, we'll see as soon as we get set in our ways, life has a funny way of smacking us with a 2×4.

Life is about searching for answers and rebelling against unjust laws, but also about adapting to our surrounding environment. That's how we survive as a species." ☺

FROM THE MIND OF CRITIC
APRIL 15TH 2017

From the mind of critic: "If life is a series of moments, snapshots frozen in time which portray good times and bad, are our days more fulfilling if we're conscious of them? Do we hang onto the good moments and let go of the bad, because we're more empowered if we're not stuffed to the gills with negativity? Do we hang onto the good, but hang onto the bad much harder, because we don't comprehend the definition of empowered? Is this due to the sheer volume of negativity permeating our every nook and cranny, making us feel like it's what we deserve? Do we let go of the bad, but cling to the good with such ferocity, that it dupes us into believing all our good days are behind us? Does this ensure no good days come in the future? We've all heard many times to not sweat the small stuff, and pay attention to the bigger picture. At some point in our life we come to realize, that it's the little things that make life worth living. The idea is that it's the little things that make up the bigger picture, and we can't cling to good things with all our might as we discard the bad. We must recognize the good for the purpose it serves, and then let go. This is when good moments flow in and out, which can only happen if we don't cling to the good moments we've had, by thinking they won't happen anymore.

If we want to continuously fill up with soul rejuvenating joy, we have to keep our eyes on what's in front of us, not simply what's behind us. Our life becomes infinitely more fulfilling, when we realize the best is yet to come." ☺

FROM THE MIND OF CRITIC

APRIL 18TH 2017

From the mind of critic: "If unexpected occurrences ruin our daily routines and plans, do we completely lose our cool? Do we get lost amidst a windstorm of self-doubt and self-preservation, making our mind spin completely out of control? Is this because our plans for everything we wanted to do, and places we wanted to go are thrown into chaos by powerful outside forces? If we're conscious enough to critically think and to expect the unexpected, do our plans change because of unforeseen circumstances? Do we adapt to our environment like many animals before us? Whether its rain, sleet, snow, wind, hurricane, tornado, a rockslide or some other unexplainable act of God, shit just happens sometimes, and we have to deal. It will test our determination to accomplish not only what we set out to do, but also what we dream of, even if we haven't yet taken the first step. We must ask ourselves how much we want to do something, and if we're willing to adapt. Once we realize we must keep moving forward to lead a fulfilling life no matter how slow a snail's pace we're travelling, we'll see nothing but nothing stops us from leading a fulfilling life, except us. No matter what, we can push forward. We just have to want to." ☺

FROM THE MIND OF CRITIC
APRIL 19TH 2017

From the mind of critic: "If we see clearly now because the rain is gone, has the rain actually stopped, or are we just able to see where the skies are clear? Do we believe the rain will never return, because it's the same for all of us, and if it stops, it stops? Do we believe it has stopped for us and not for others, causing us to discard our rain hats, coats, boots and umbrellas? Is it like a cartoon rain cloud that only rains on others, while we sit under a beautiful blue sky with birds chirping? Can we see clearly not because the rain has stopped or permanently disappeared, but because the rain has no effect on us? Is this because we've activated the most impermeable connections known to man, a critically thinking brain, a loving heart and a driven soul? It's so interesting when we read, watch or hear something when we're older, that was entertaining when we were younger. We can pull a completely different meaning from something using the same exact language. The easiest examples are cartoons, books and movies, but we also see the definitions of old sayings change as we gain life experience. If we can see clearly now, we must ask ourselves why? Has our definition of clear changed? Has the ferocity of the rain changed? Has our sight changed? Once we realize the rain as well our critical thoughts change simultaneously, we'll see that even though we can see clearly now, the rain isn't permanently gone.

The moment we believe the rain won't ever come back, is the exact moment when it does. Clarity of thought is only achieved through perseverance, not stagnation." ☺

FROM THE MIND OF CRITIC
APRIL 20TH 2017

From the mind of critic: "If plants need water and sun to live, what type of fertilizer is needed to thrive? Are all plants hungry for the same nutrients, looking for a universal elixir to make them big, strong, vibrant, productive and help them serve their purpose? Are all plants hungry for different nutrients, looking for the magic that works for their unique needs, which will make them big, strong, vibrant, productive and help them serve their purpose? There are universal truths that make us the same, we all need food, water and shelter to survive. Clothing while socially imperative won't immediately harm us if we go without. There are also special truths which are representative of the unique snowflakes we are. We all come from different environments and generations, with different backgrounds, upbringings, beliefs and financial resources. As such, different things reach us for different reasons. Once we realize infinite happenings reach us for infinite reasons, we'll see expecting all people to respond to the same stimuli is more than a fools' errand, it's a collectively detrimental act. All plants might require different fertilizers to thrive, but they all need fertilizer. What makes us different actually makes us the same." ☺

FROM THE MIND OF CRITIC
APRIL 21ST 2017

From the mind of critic: "If cheap doesn't always mean worse, and expensive doesn't always mean better, what's the ballast point? If poor and homeless doesn't always mean inferior, and rich and influential don't always mean superior, what's the precedent? Are we doing ourselves wrong by looking for a black and white rock of Gibraltar, an end all be all scale to decipher if our judgements are correct? Are we taking two steps back if we validate our judgements, solidifying that we don't want to learn new things? Do we think we have all the answers, and everyone who agrees is our friend, and everyone who disagrees is our enemy? Stereotypes, labels, epithets, nicknames and assumptions are used to simplify our complex world. So much information, events and opportunities flash by on a daily basis, that we have to form them in a way our brains comprehend. What shoves our progress backward, is labeling something and then never asking questions again, thinking we have it all figured out. Once we realize most of our assumptions end up opposite of what we think, we'll see labels don't free our thoughts, they stop us from thinking. If life is learned as we go, we'll never have everything figured out. Labels inhibit evolution, they don't help it along. Moving forward includes critical thinking, not blind assumptions." ☺

FROM THE MIND OF CRITIC

APRIL 22ND 2017

From the mind of critic: "If we're used to shoving materials in the garbage disposal, has emptying it even crossed our mind? Do we believe our disposal is a bottomless pit, lifting the burden of discerning what we throw away? Do we understand no disposal is designed to withstand endless amounts of garbage, causing us to think about what we're throwing away, and what we're using that'll have to be tossed later? Whether it's a garbage disposal, a rug or a bottomless pit, there are countless devices, metaphors and made up nonsense we utilize daily. Sometimes we have household trash, sometimes we have dinner remains, and sometimes inhumane acts we have to hide. We've all done things we aren't proud of, and things we regret not covering up. We must learn what to avoid, so we don't keep making the same mistakes. We might become better at covering up indiscretions, taking our misdeeds to the next level. Once we realize we all have secrets, we'll see exactly why politicians get caught, and understand if we had their power and influence, we'd feel just as above the law. If our garbage disposal explodes, we either get a bigger one by getting elected to office, or become better human citizens by holding the world accountable, by holding ourselves accountable. All schemes are discovered eventually, we gain peace of mind the second we start living honestly." ☺

FROM THE MIND OF CRITIC
APRIL 25TH 2017

From the mind of critic: "If we display a blank stare at different times of the day, is it always for the same reason? Do we stare off because we're happy with how things are, and how much better things will get? Do we stare because we're sad, and can't believe a tragedy happened? Do we see what we're staring at? Do we not feel happy or sad but focused when we stare, because we're developing the next creative idea to enlighten the world? Do we stare out of trauma, because part of us has died? Do we realize deviating stares happen for all different reasons, even though they appear identical? Do we remain oblivious to the difference between stares, thinking there must be something wrong with the starrer? All of us are unique snowflakes with unique experiences, brought on by unique environments and unique upbringings. If we can't judge a book's content's by the cover, how can we judge a person with a look we deem not appropriate or unwarranted? Once we realize infinite stares appear the same, except for minutely subtle differences only visible when a person's character is known, we'll see until we truly know somebody, projecting our thoughts, fear, emotions and hate onto others is a fool's errand; with us being the fool. Blank stares might appear blank, but are teeming with emotion that we only see when we look deeper. We do ourselves a lot of good when we don't rely on life's cliff notes." ☺

FROM THE MIND OF CRITIC
APRIL 26TH 2017

From the mind of critic: "If we believe growth flows from the top down and not the bottom up, what evidence are we relying on to prove this assumption? Are we relying on generations of economic theory from Ayn Rand, Milton Friedman and Adam Smith that says we'll have infinite wealth when we unshackle the economy? What proof do we have that the rich will provide more jobs, by spending their newly found wealth? Have we seen examples of rich friends contributing to job growth, specifically because they're already in an outrageously high financial position? Do these friends believe they're not rich enough, and if they do receive more money, they can economically contribute like never before? Are moneyed classes sucking up all the natural resources they can, because they can? Hypocrisy is a funny word, every human has aspects of it, just some more than others. What's even funnier is when people deflect criticism and blame for unseen, nefarious reasons. Sometimes we twist facts, and sometimes we make up facts. Maybe we discover that for every dollar we give to the bottom of the income scale, $1.70 goes back into the economy. Maybe we find that the first thing people do who get money when they don't have it, is spend it. Maybe we find that rich people become rich because they don't spend money back into the economy, and instead pay fewer taxes.

Maybe this means less revenue into the government because the burden was kept from major campaign contributors. Maybe we discover deficit hawks only exist on issues that don't concern them. Maybe we find people are Democrats when they don't have money and Republicans when they do. Once we realize greed exists at the top and the bottom, we'll see that to stop fraud, we must stop it everywhere, at all levels. If we actually want to fix issues instead of endlessly yakking about them, we'll base our laws on statistics not slippery slopes. Growth flows from the bottom up like a potted plant, not from the top down like no plant ever." ☺

FROM THE MIND OF CRITIC
APRIL 27TH 2017

From the mind of critic: "If a road has traffic moving in opposite directions even though it's the same road, is there a way to make those traveling in opposite directions, travel in the same direction? Is it feasible let alone technically possible to form a one way road, when drivers feel compelled with the very fiber of their being to drive in opposite directions? Should we force drivers to drive in one direction, because we believe the roads will be freer and fairer, if all of us drive in the same direction? Should we specifically build roads we can drive in opposite directions on? Will roads be more peaceful, if we drive in the direction that takes us where we want to go? All relationships whether platonic, romantic, workplace, familial or recreational are two way streets. The give and take amidst the chaos of life is a lot to handle, and impossible to quantify. We all take different roads, paths and trails toward the same basic place. Once we realize these different paths must work in unison not against each other, we'll see none of us will truly get where we want, unless we all do. The laws of physics demand that roads head in multiple opposite directions. That is unless we want to crash into each other, preventing any of us from moving forward." ☺

FROM THE MIND OF CRITIC
APRIL 28TH 2017

From the mind of critic: "If everything we need to know we learned in kindergarten, why should we learn anything new? Do these lessons represent the pillars of life, and striving past them represents how much they don't matter? Are these pillars the very foundation of our character, which we don't discard as we journey, but use them to grow into the humans we always thought we were? Lots of changes happen on a daily basis, something every generation has experienced. As our world shifts from the comfortable rut we've settled into, it can be scary to deal with things we've never had to before. Sometimes these are issues we've never seen, or issues we've ignored. However, they appear new when they stand up to slap us in the face. When this happens, it's important to remember rudimentary human interaction. What we learned in kindergarten, getting back to nature, however we describe it, its part and parcel of the same concept. Treating others like we'd like to be treated, remembering to share and balancing work and play, if woven into our adult routines would fix most of our ingrained issues. Have we forgotten how basic and uncomplicated solutions are? The less complication, and more love and understanding we utilize, the more beautiful life becomes. We are the people we've been waiting for." ☺

FROM THE MIND OF CRITIC
APRIL 29TH 2017

From the mind of critic: "If a rose grows through the concrete, is it stronger than other roses? Will it grow due to its undying, unrelenting and courageous compassion to throw off the restrictive shackles of concrete? Does the rose grow not because of the great and authentic strength it possesses, but because the concrete is porous, as compared to the unbreakable facade it portrays? The world can be harsh, dark and so physically and emotionally draining, it seems we'll always be fiercely held back from reaching our true potential. The world can also be welcoming, light filled and so emotionally and spiritually uplifting, it seem like we'll be supported and gently pushed toward our true potential. This can happen when we allow ourselves to open up to the beauty of the world. It's all about perspective, where we see light and dark. Sometimes light and dark happen regardless of our perspective, just to test our soul's fortitude. This is when we have to do inner work, and discover what drives us, and what we're passionate about. Once we find our passion, we'll go after it no matter what light or dark we're shown. Once we realize the conscious use of this energy dispels the illusion of strength elites display, we'll see that using what drives us to better the planet and the people on it, is exactly how we evolve into the species we've always dreamed of being.

The pen is mightier than the sword, as the rose is mightier than the concrete. The more positive and collective growth we gain, the more cracks appear in the wall meant to box us all in." ☺

FROM THE MIND OF CRITIC
MAY 2ND 2017

From the mind of critic: "If we take our rights for granted, because the battles that spawned them took place long before we could have taken part, do we not comprehend people currently fighting for their rights? Do we paint them as complainers, even though they're simply standing up for what they believe in like our forefathers did? Have we not needed to stand up because our social, political, religious or financial status was locked in by generations of pawning off responsibilities, completely removing the human aspect? Are we so sucked into surviving our own narcissism, that until something truly threatens our lives, we won't lift a finger to help anybody outside our bubble? We aren't okay with somebody taking our rights away and turning us into some third world dictatorship. We aren't okay with a 30 year ruler that institutes bread lines and daily blackouts, because they've sucked the nation's coffers dry. If we're not okay with that, why are we okay with somebody else having their rights discarded, creating a third world situation where they are forced to live. We all come from the same basic place, none of us succeed until we all succeed, we all do better when we all do better. However we slice it, we all have to live on this planet together. Once we realize all wars have been fought by the poor to benefit the rich, that all of us are immigrants, and that none of us are an island, we'll see we've all had to fight for our rights at some point.

Just because we've had things hard, doesn't mean somebody else should be forced to have things just as hard; but when they are, we shouldn't get on their case for doing the same exact thing we did. The second we take our rights for granted, is the second they disappear. If we don't fight to get them back, they'll be permanently gone. Do we practice what we preach, or do we preach what we practice?" ☺

FROM THE MIND OF CRITIC

MAY 3RD 2017

From the mind of critic: "If garbage trucks take our garbage away once a week, does it give us a false sense of security and morality that our garbage has disappeared forever? Do we believe discarding refuse once prevents it from coming back? Do we believe paying somebody to take our trash away, prevents us from having to deal? Does the compacted trash a garbage truck unloads at the end of a route, represent a collective that rids us all of what we don't need? Are we getting rid of all different things, or just different versions of the same thing? Letting go is the greatest thing we can do to prolong the life of our heart and mind. We must be vigilantly on the lookout for things we can let go of and hold onto. Letting go is a constant process, not a one off. Only we can make the decisions for what's best for us, and what will lead to a more fulfilling and productive life. For good things to flow in and out of our lives like rain, we have to let go of what doesn't serve us, specifically to make room for what does. Once we realize we have to let go of negativity all day every day, not once a day, week, month or year, we'll see we can't pay somebody to let go or take things away for us, we must do it ourselves and not just portray the illusion. Paying somebody to take our trash is helpful, but not as satisfying as tossing it ourselves. It keeps us conscious of what we're throwing away. The key to a joyfully fulfilling life is to make everyday trash day." ☺

FROM THE MIND OF CRITIC
MAY 4TH 2017

From the mind of critic: "If we've ever told our kids or other young people, "do as I say not as I do" are we ceding responsibility of our actions? Are we holding others to a higher standard than ourselves, because we don't think we can reach that higher standard? Are we looking for future scapegoats by encouraging people to pay closer attention to our words than actions, because we're complicit in the action? Do we honestly want others to live their lives more joyfully than ours, specifically because we're firm believers in leaving the world and its inhabitants better than it was found? Accountability and humanism can solve most of the problems we have as a society. What we forget sometimes is to help ourselves, after spending all day helping others. Maybe we feel we don't deserve help, or it's too hard to look internally for answers, because we have to be accountable, just like we're asking of others. All of us have heard the old quote, "be the change we want to see". If we spend all our time ejecting empty words not tied to actions, we'll end up like the crazy preacher on the street corner. We'll scream and yell all day, but the only people who listen will be the police when they tell us to move along. Wanting others to live better, achieve more and strive further is a noble mission, which makes the world a better place by simply making the attempt.

However, if we expect others to do things we see as below us, unimportant or easily ignorable, we'll devolve our entire species by spreading false information, dressed in a caring and tolerant aioli. "Do as I say not as I do" aren't words to live by, they're words that make us complacent and apathetic. What will evolve us, complacency or vigilance?" ☺

FROM THE MIND OF CRITIC
MAY 5TH 2017

From the mind of critic: "If we go through drivers-education, a DMV written test, a DMV drive test, and pass them all to earn a restricted license for the first year, does it guarantee good driving? Does extensive study of rules and regulations before passing tests guarantee we'll never get a ticket or get in an accident? Will we always drive safe, sane and sober with other crazies on the road? Does extensive study which produces a satisfactory grade give us a false sense of security, because although we've read what it means to be a good driver, we haven't experienced its real life applications? Will we take undue risks when we otherwise wouldn't? Just because we've read, studied and tested extensively, doesn't guarantee life will turn out roses. At the same time, just because we've had many real life experiences, doesn't mean testing and schooling will come easy either. Balancing school smarts and street smarts, is one of the most important aspects of a complete human being. We can't fully experience and know something, until we live that experience. Once we realize schooling alone does not an expert make, we'll see unless we critically think about how our past, present and future fit together, we'll never be the experts we claim. To ensure our 2×4 moment is a love tap and not a pile-driver, we must admit we don't know everything, and are open to learning as much as possible.

Driver training is a good thing, but is only effective when it leads to more questions. The more knowledge we gain, the more knowledge we discover we've yet to learn." ☺

FROM THE MIND OF CRITIC
MAY 9TH 2017

From the mind of critic: "If we're known for standing up for what we believe, do we have to keep up a certain persona to deem ourselves worthy of praise? If we're standing up for the rights of our culture, ethnicity or gender, and we mix and mingle with another culture, ethnicity or gender, do we feel like we're letting our people down by not giving them a chance? Do we understand the intricacies of the human psyche, and gravitate toward consciously positive and justice filled people? Do we realize "our people" might only be upset, because they haven't had black and white enough truth to prove that "others" might help "them?" We as humans don't believe monolithically, we believe a million different things for a million different reasons. When we drill deeper within our ethnicity, culture, religion or movement, none of us believe the same. If we disagree with somebody in our group for associating with another group, are we doing it out of pride? Do we think our people are better than other people? Once we realize equal rights mean inclusion in the mainstream, we'll see living what we preach is the reason why we preach, not just to be heard. We should all stand up for what we believe. The moment we put our ideas into practice, is the moment we evolve. We think to talk and talk to act, we can't let others who haven't made that connection bring us down." ☺

FROM THE MIND OF CRITIC
MAY 10TH 2017

From the mind of critic: "When we walk out our front door to start our day, do we look for other open doors to walk through? Do doors just appear, beckoning us to walk through, or do we have to hunt and search? If one door opens, does another close? Do all available doors appear so numerous, that we have to know ourselves to choose the one which suits us? Are some doors hidden, only revealing themselves after we've dealt with adversity, fed our passion, learned a certain lesson, or got out of our way long enough to realize opportunities aren't just for other people? Many doors, windows and keyholes will present themselves whether or not we're ready. At the same time, many walls, vaults and missing doorknobs will present themselves whether or not we're prepared. The key is to stay open, balancing the good and the bad. If we analyze it all, we'll know what's uplifting, what's destructive, and what's not worth our time. Once we realize we can't guarantee when good or bad doors appear, but can greatly increase our probability for success if we learn what we're looking for and what our passion is, we'll see that truly knowing ourselves is the best path forward. Whether we expect doors to open or not, we must be prepared to walk through. We do that by opening the door to our soul, and getting to know our true selves."☺

FROM THE MIND OF CRITIC

MAY 11TH 2017

From the mind of critic: "If at first we don't succeed, do we try again? Do we succeed on our 4th, 8th or 12th try? What about our 200th or 500th? Do we gain success specifically because of our vigilantly courageous determination? Do we gain success not simply because of determination, but hard work, focus, consciousness, understanding, justice and love for our fellow man? I've always heard success is in the eye of the beholder, which means we determine what success means. Whatever success looks like to us, might not be what it looks like for somebody else. At the same time, we might not be able to see success meant for us, specifically because we think it's meant for somebody else. We've all hit rough patches where we try really hard for something, and it just doesn't happen, or in the way we expect. We must remember if we want something to happen, and we put in massive effort, what matters is that it happens, not its form. We aren't guaranteed success, but we aren't guaranteed failure either. We are guaranteed utter regret however if we don't try. No matter what form success takes, it's still success." ☺

FROM THE MIND OF CRITIC
MAY 12TH 2017

From the mind of critic: "If we trim our fruit trees in the winter so branches grow back thicker and stronger in the spring, do we expect these runners to automatically spring up? Do we prune small branches and leave big ones because new smaller growth always springs from bigger growth? Does new growth only happen when the stars align, and planetary conditions are just right? Putting in hard work and effort provides a much better chance for success, but it's not guaranteed. Knowing success isn't guaranteed shouldn't stop us from putting in hard work. Environments, people, thoughts and actions have to align for success to happen, but since we don't know what perfect conditions look like, we also don't know in what form success will spring forth. We must remember the more preparation we put in, the stronger our foundation. We'll see how the house built on that strong foundation is interconnected to all other houses on the block, neighborhood, city, state, country and world. Trimming fruit trees has to be done in the right conditions, and with the right technique; lopping off random branches will kill the tree. If we think about how what we're doing affects everything else, the tree will not only grow, but it'll thrive. Once we consciously realize nobody gets it perfect, the more successful we'll be." ☺

FROM THE MIND OF CRITIC
MAY 13TH 2017

From the mind of critic: "When we're at a coffee shop deciding between light and dark roast, do we ever mix the two to create medium? Do we thoroughly enjoy the taste of light and dark together instead of medium roast, because the natural mixing of the two provides an authentic flavor which medium roast is unable to mimic? Do we prefer medium roast because the mixing has already been done, instead of us making the conscious decision to mix? Whether we prefer lightness, darkness, medium-ness or have no preference, we're making choices about what kind of coffee we like, what kind of emotional outlook we utilize and the ethnicity of people we feel comfortable around. We run into trouble when we get hung up on type, instead of the actual thing. If we like coffee we should drink it, no matter the type. Whether we do or don't understand our emotional outlook, we should always build ourselves up, no matter what shade of consciousness we come from. If we like people, we should treat them with dignity, respect and love no matter their melanin level. Having preferences isn't inherently a bad thing. We just have to be careful those preferences don't hurt, harm or hate others based on ignorance. Mixing, matching and creating make life interesting and keeps our species evolving. The less judgement and more understanding we carry, the more we move forward instead of backward." ☺

FROM THE MIND OF CRITIC
MAY 16TH 2017

From the mind of critic: "Is fighting for peace, like loving for war? Is committing violence till our enemies can't challenge us anymore, just as ridiculous as believing random acts of kindness will get people so angry, their only thought will be to kill each other? Can things be ridiculous but not surprising, because crazy off the wall things have become so prevalent, they've been normalized? Double speak, double talk, double think and hypocrisy have been around since the dawn of man. So we shouldn't be surprised when we're duped by phrases created by sinister intent. At the same time, if we don't stand up and speak about the start of humanities downfall, duplicitous thoughts, statements and actions will happen with more frequency and ferocity, until they guarantee humanities downfall. How do we stave this off? We realize the real world application of fighting is war, while peace is love by understanding what actions we're currently taking. Random acts of kindness, treating others how we'd like to be treated, and remembering to share when we have a lot and others have little, is the love that cultivates peace. Love creates peace, and peace ends war. If we really want to stop the apocalypse, we need to stop trying to kill our enemies into submission, and start loving them into submission. We start evolving when we realize fighting and loving are two totally different things." ☺

FROM THE MIND OF CRITIC
MAY 17TH 2017

From the mind of critic: "If words mean everything and nothing at the same time, is it any wonder we have trouble communicating? If our words can't be taken more seriously than actions, does it matter what anybody says? How do we find balance between everything and nothing, when the middle ground is completely indecipherable? Do we take everything on a case by case basis, and realize pre-conceived notions get us absolutely nowhere? Do we have etched in stone rules with no exceptions, where crazy words, phrases and concepts coming from somebody we like is chalked up under things we can't take seriously, while honest words, phrases and concepts are taken as the gospel? Many things in life have to be balanced, free and work time, personal and business and diet just to name a few. We run into problems when we try to balance something, and it spells to the letter how unbalanced somebody else thinks it is. We might think crazy shouldn't be believed from our guy, but damn if we're not ready to lock our opponent up for saying the same exact thing. We must ask ourselves if we want to live our lives draped in hypocrisy, or realism. We might never figure out a black and white answer to whether words matter, the best we can do is hold our friends and enemies to the same standards. Once we're all measured by the same ruler, we'll see how similar we really are." ☺

FROM THE MIND OF CRITIC
MAY 18TH 2017

From the mind of critic: "If we're whistling down the street because nothing will break our stride, but then see a piece of trash, do we pick it up? If our attitude is nothing will stop us from getting where we want to go, do we purposely slow our journey to beautify our path, and all others who come after? Do we purposely pass by trash as we saunter by, because we think somebody will pick it up, allowing us to scoot further ahead? It's very common within the human condition to watch out for ourselves, and make sure nothing upsets the productive, uplifting and fulfilling plans we've made. What we must remember is that just because something is common, doesn't mean it's beneficial. While we all want to get somewhere, we all need help along the way. If we pass somebody whether physically or metaphorically who needs help, we should help them if we can, specifically because we could be in their position. Once we realize that just because our stride is broken doesn't mean we're slowed down, we'll see that if we adjust our plans, it builds character by making us step outside of ourselves. Waving at and helping random people, reminds us of the humanism we've lost, but also how easily it returns. Helping and/or beautifying is better done by us, now. If we count on somebody else, are we okay with them counting on us?" ☺

FROM THE MIND OF CRITIC
MAY 19TH 2017

From the mind of critic: "If our old, haggard dresser is ready to completely break down, do we set it by the side of the road for the trash man, after we've smashed it to smithereens? Do we scour yard sales for a cheap and easy replacement, attempting to cover up our self-inflicted destruction? Do we trudge down to the hardware store for sand paper, stain and lacquer to refinish a dresser that's a shadow of its former self because of years of neglect and apathy? In the crazy times we're currently forced to live in, the freedom and equality America was based on seems like a distant memory. Not that we've ever fully handled issues of race, class, religion, abortion, guns or gays, which are all reasons we have Donald Trump as president. Since everything is out in the open, all the cracks, holes and flaws are available for us to witness. Given that we've all seen American flaws, do we feel it has been so corrupt for so long, we're better off blowing up the system and starting over? Should we give up on the American dream that has never been fully realized? Do we force the system to be better, by putting in the work? Once we realize we don't have to destroy to improve, we'll see clean slate thinking as the easy way out. Fixing an old dresser might be a lot of work, but it's more fulfilling because we fixed what caused the deterioration, instead of buying another dresser, and kicking the can down the road once again." ☺

FROM THE MIND OF CRITIC
MAY 20TH 2017

From the mind of critic: "How do we know everything happens for a reason, if that reason isn't translatable into any human dialect? Do we have faith in a higher power or some other unseen force, which provides an explanatory reason before anything actually happens? Do we know some reasons are yet to be translatable but will become so, the more consciousness and life experience we allow ourselves to gain? Does this future knowledge provide motivation needed to trudge forward, to find the needle amongst the field of haystacks? Many things in life are unexplainable for a plethora of reasons. How we react to this knowledge, is directly correlated to our view of the world and its inhabitants. There's a reason everything happens, some are terrible, despicable and soul ripping, while some are joyous, beautiful and soul nurturing. Some reasons certainly aren't explainable yet, and some might not ever be. Once we realize the monumental disservice we do to our personal evolution by trying to find the easy answers to life's events, we'll see we might not comprehend everything that happens, but the more consciously we look for answers, the more authentic those answers and reasons will appear. There's a reason everything happens for a reason, which happens to be our life's journey." ☺

FROM THE MIND OF CRITIC

MAY 23RD 2017

From the mind of critic: "If clear, hold and build is employed regularly as a military strategy, does it work as a civilian strategy? Soldiers are taught to clear enemies out of an area, hold by defending against enemies trying to wrestle control back, and then build the area into a vibrant and productive community. Can civilians be taught to clear negativity, sabotage and self-imposed roadblocks, hold by defending against negativity and sabotage from stealing self-confidence and love. Then build their mind and psyche by working their passion, filling their cup with beauty and kindness, and living and enjoying each day to its fullest by being open and honest about what's in front of them. Is military and civilian life completely separate, because civilian life is about humanizing to become better people, while military life is about dehumanizing people in war as an absolute last resort? Humans become soldiers and vice versa, just like politicians. We clean up politics by cleaning up our personal life, same with the military. However like life, we have to let go of the bad and keep the good. Becoming conscious, defending that consciousness and then building on it will help us achieve our dreams. Where we run into problems is when we try to hold and defend our new found consciousness, and build on it by being more open and fulfilled, before we clear out our clutter.

Once we realize letting go isn't a onetime thing but a constant process, we'll see we can't wait till all our negativity is gone before we raise our consciousness, or we'll waiting for Godot till the cows come home. Clear, hold and build can work in civilian life, we just can't wait to clear everything before we start holding and building, or we'll never evolve." ☺

FROM THE MIND OF CRITIC

MAY 24TH 2017

From the mind of critic: "If mechanics are good at diagnosing and fixing car problems, is it because they studied long and hard in hopes of one day becoming successful? Are mechanics born without car knowledge, and have to consciously think, seek out, apply and practice to see how much it improves the overall health and longevity of the car? Are mechanics special human beings amongst a small group, which have been tasked with not only fixing their own car, but friends, family, and acquaintances as well? Do they realize after much heartache and strife that the vast majority of humans don't care to work on their car, always expecting somebody else to do it for them? It always is, always has been and always will be true that we know ourselves better than anybody. However, we can always become more knowledgeable. If we want to know how we tick, what we like, what we don't like, where we'd like to go or why we feel sad, unproductive and like we're not worthy, we must do inner work. If something is wrong with us physically, we go to a doctor, something wrong mentally, we go to a shrink. Once we realize that we need to analyze ourselves before we seek outside help, we'll see the better we know ourselves, the more we can fix our own issues. The more we fix our own issues, the less we ask for help.

That's not to say we'll never need help. A facet of true knowledge is not being so proud as to not ask for help when it's needed. We must remember we aren't born with knowledge, it's gained through experience. To gain that experience, we must allow it to happen. To live a more fulfilling life, we have to consciously act. Mechanics are good at fixing cars, because they consciously try to fix cars. The more conscious we are, the more joyful we are, it's that simple." ☺

FROM THE MIND OF CRITIC
MAY 25TH 2017

From the mind of critic: "If good things can feel bad and bad things can feel good, how do we decide what's uplifting and what's detrimental? If the truth hurts beyond words, yet ignorance breeds joy that's indescribable, does being truthful with our feelings make us sadistic human beings who take pleasure in torturing ourselves? Does being truthful hurt because it requires critical and pragmatic thought, instead of staying in the comfortable rut we've built, where we don't have to think or act, only react? The truth hurts is such an old concept, that all of us have experienced it multiple times whether or not it was something we did. Sometimes we shy away from true feelings, because we're scared of outcomes. Sometimes we're so close to achieving something we want we can taste it, but once we're truthful, we get pulled further away. We then question whether we're being honest about what we want, or are self-sabotaging this wonderful, awesome and amazing thing, because it's only 85% of what we want. This is when we must question if that 15% of things overshadows the 85% of things we love. Does this 15% include what drives us, what we're passionate about, and what brings us joy?

When 85% of something is the best thing that has happened to us in a long time, but doesn't include what we're passionate about, nor the intellectual, philosophical, political, historical and bettering the world conversation which makes us high, is it still the best thing? Life can be very tricky, meanings and definitions quickly flip. The truth might hurt, but pain is temporary, before giving way to long term joy. Critical thought and self-reflection is the only path forward, unless we take a false path backward once we discover truth." ☺

FROM THE MIND OF CRITIC
MAY 26TH 2017

From the mind of critic: "If a tree loses its leaves, flowers and small branches in the fall, does it die? Is autumn about losing the old, and clearing the way for new growth in the spring? Is the tree just delaying the inevitable, dying in little bits before its ultimate demise? We all shed things which don't serve us from time to time, with or without our knowledge. Like a snake that sheds its skin or a dog that sheds its fur, so to must we shed our insecurities, negativity and ignorance to make room for new growth. These new sprouts not only keep us fresh, vibrant and with it, they also keep us evolving and adapting as the environment changes around us. In the business world, they say you're either growing or dying. In the human world, we might not die from not growing, but we will wilt into a nothingness soup of insignificance and regret. We all want to grow and become the people of our dreams. To make that possible we must eject everything dragging us down, specifically to make room for everything that builds us up. A tree might lose foliage, but new growth will be brighter and more vibrant if allowed to flourish." ☺

FROM THE MIND OF CRITIC
MAY 30TH 2017

From the mind of critic: "Is money the root of all evil, or is evil the root of all money? Does money always come from evil deeds? Does evil always come from the procurement of money? Is it always one way, or the other? Do reactions change because of history, upbringings, moods, and ego and self-esteem levels? Money exists as a tangible entity, because we have faith it exists. If we didn't put our faith in little pieces of plastic or green paper, it would be shells and rocks, or some other natural resource we assigned value to so we could gauge wealth and social class. Evil exists because it balances out good. Evil doesn't disappear if we lose faith in it, but does shrink into insignificance. Maybe separating people into rich and poor is an evil act, an act done with money and wealth in mind. The more people who are controlled, the more money is made. Maybe the real issue isn't money and evil, but being human or inhuman. Once we realize money can be used for good, and allow humanism to be unleashed amongst exponential darkness, we'll see that as long as we're human to each other, money and evil will never take over the lightest part of our soul. Money is only the root of evil, if evil is the intent." ☺

FROM THE MIND OF CRITIC
MAY 31ST 2017

From the mind of critic: "If we know our plants won't live without water, but we don't have any because of drought, do we take what little water others have for ourselves? Do we try to fix the drought, by conserving fluids we receive through crude filters and flanges? Do we try to usher in rain through not only prayers and rain dances, but by being courageously vigilant in finding why drought happens, and what we can be done so it doesn't happen again? When we find ourselves un-knowledgeable about a certain topic, event, religion or culture, there are many paths we can take. We can get mad at people with more knowledge, because we see them as being pompous, jerk know-it-alls. We can get mad at people who have less knowledge, because we view them as talentless, know nothings. We can also see others at various knowledge levels, and understand if we want to gain more knowledge, we don't have to take, we share. Once we realize we never have to feel threatened or intimidated when comparing smarts, we'll see labeling, separating and grouping ourselves along ideological and intellectual lines, makes us all dumber. Our plants can't live without water, like we can't live without knowledge. We just have to remember that whether we're watering our plants or our souls to sustain life, to replenish doesn't take away, it adds. If we admit we don't care if we know stuff, we're admitting we don't care if we're controlled." ☺

FROM THE MIND OF CRITIC

JUNE 1ST 2017

From the mind of critic: "Whether we like burnt toast or light toast, we still like toast right? Whether we like black coffee or coffee with cream, we still like coffee right? Whether we like devil's food cake or angel's food cake, we still like cake right? Whether we like chocolate ice cream or vanilla, we still like ice cream right? Some would argue our whole system of government is based on hypocritical designs. Some would argue all organisms have trouble with adaptation, mutation and evolution. Whatever side we find ourselves on, we must remember we're all human, and all going after the same basic things. Maybe we think it's okay to put somebody down, for liking a different form of the same thing we like. Whether it's an issue of saying one thing and doing another, or ignorance of the "other", we wade through our own hypocrisy on a daily basis. That's not to say we shouldn't express what we like, quite the contrary. We should express what we like. It not only makes life worth living, but also instills in us the ability to stand up for what we believe. We run into trouble when we think what we believe, is more important than what somebody else believes, not realizing we're two sides of the same coin. If we're so sick and tired of hypocrisy that it makes us ill, do we realize the cure is continuously looking in the mirror?" ☺

FROM THE MIND OF CRITIC
JUNE 2ND 2017

From the mind of critic: "If we're not supposed to judge a book by its cover, but the cover entices us to read the book, how do we find balance? Do we not judge a book by its whole cover but only its title, so we're not judging the outside packaging, but the name of the packaging? Do we look at the cover without judgment, because we're saving our judgement for the books interior? Is there a tangible difference between judgement and prejudgment? Whether we judge somebody before getting to know them or after, we're still judging. Every day we face being pegged as something we're not. The problem with judging somebody by the content of their character is we're still judging. Regardless of the type of person somebody is or their beliefs, judgement is way above any of our pay grades. Yes, there are good, bad and middle of the road people out there. However, unless we know every single thing about somebody, including all their idiosyncrasies which they themselves might not be fully aware of, we have no place to judge. If our collective goals in life are to treat others how we'd like to be treated, then we must treat everyone with love and understanding, because we'll never know their full life experience. It's not so much that we shouldn't judge a book by its cover, we shouldn't judge a book, period." ☺

FROM THE MIND OF CRITIC
JUNE 3RD 2017

From the mind of critic: "If polls show a majority of people support something, that the democratically elected leader of their country doesn't, does it prove the people vote in polls, but not elections? Do we love complaining to anybody who will listen, but are too lazy to take action? Do we all want our egos stroked? Do we care if we're heard every four years on the first Tuesday in November, because we're just checking a box? Many of us don't see a point in voting, and don't think it matters. There are many countries around the world whose populations vote 70-80% of the time, electing leaders who espouse direct policy priorities the population agrees with. If we in America voted at the 70 or 80% level instead of the 30% we do, many of our ingrained generational issues would be solved, because we'd be standing up on a consistent basis, instead of spewing our opinion to an ego-stroker. We all have a right to complain whether we vote or not, that's what makes us American. We just can't expect our complaints to have any resolution, if we aren't willing to follow up. Solutions require action, not simply complaining." ☺

FROM THE MIND OF CRITIC
JUNE 6TH 2017

From the mind of critic: "If we're riding in a boat and it springs a leak, do we keep riding along oblivious to the leak? Do we know about the leak, but think it'll fix itself if we go about our business and pretend it isn't there? Do we try to fix the leak by drilling more holes in the boat, hoping the new leaks take attention away from the old ones? Do we fix the leak by plugging it, because we know too many leaks make a boat sink? No government is air tight, no matter how much officials claim. The more leaks are mentioned, the greater possibility leaks exist. When nefarious, criminal, evil and despicable acts are committed by office holders or those who aspire to be, the more they scheme to cover them up. The more sinister the scheme, the more likely somebody's consciousness isn't going to let them continue, which causes leaks and spilled beans. The office holders then deny the leak, doing everything they can to distract. This distraction is done by leaking other things, to pull attention away from the original leaks. Like the three stooges however, water doesn't drain by creating more leaks. It makes the boat sink under a wall of water. We can address leaks by fixing what caused them. The more we pay attention to what's in front of us, the less time we spend on a leaky boat. Do we want to float on a sea of truth, or drown in its vastness?" ☺

FROM THE MIND OF CRITIC
JUNE 7TH 2017

From the mind of critic: "If we make a better door than a window, do we make a better window than a door? Does our inexperience at window making, overshadow our experience at door making, causing us to cocoon in a windowless and door-less room? Is this a physical room, or a room in our minds? Are we great at making windows and doors for other people, but when it comes to ourselves, we can't nail two boards together? Opportunities, lessons and new beginnings present themselves all the time, whether we're paying attention or not. They can be detrimental or uplifting, depending on our outlook and self-esteem. A window might be constructed before the door. Sometimes the window we look through can be a crutch, so we never have to walk through the door. The door itself might be nailed shut, tricking us into believing we can stroll through. Then again everything might be a pipe dream. Doors, windows, locked cabinets and blocked hallways can be metaphors with a million variables, and a million more explanations and outcomes depending on our determination and life experience. Like job experience is gained on the job, life experience is gained through living. The less we concentrate on words, and more on concepts, the more we'll see our life dramatically improve.

Words aren't everything, but without them, how would we learn anything? Windows and doors can be passages or road blocks, it's our choice." ☺

FROM THE MIND OF CRITIC
JUNE 13TH 2017

From the mind of critic: "If authority figures drone into our brains that "we should do as they say not as they do", is it any wonder we don't trust authority? If we're told lies so flagrantly often, do we internalize the notion of "it is what it is"? Do we rely on emotions, when facts cease to exist? Do we still believe in facts, even if proof of their non-existence is manufactured by those who profit off of our gullibility? Humans will always try to take advantage of others, but will also love each other if given the opportunity. Sometimes we block these chances, sometimes authority blocks them. Once we realize that taking everything with a grain of salt doesn't mean everything is a lie, we'll see just because there are fields of haystacks, doesn't mean there aren't any needles. Trust of authority must be earned, but if it has been earned, we must give it the benefit of the doubt." ☺

FROM THE MIND OF CRITIC
JUNE 14TH 2017

From the mind of critic: "If we don't know what we've been told, are we curious enough to ask questions? Do we go along with the status quo, because people more powerful and influential made plans we have no control over? Do we understand that when we don't know something, we can ask questions to clear up inconsistencies and misinformation? Propagandic rhetoric floods our cortex on a daily basis. People tell us all the time things we do know, things we don't, and things they are unaware of our knowledge level on. The more gullible, uninformed, apathetic and complacent we are, the more we'll be controlled by unseen forces, whose power seems impenetrable. Once we realize people power will always crush elite power by way of sheer numbers, we'll see the only way for us to unite is by asking questions, and deleting blind faith from our action plan. We might know what we've been told, but unless we enjoy being a doormat, we must start asking why." ☺

FROM THE MIND OF CRITIC
JUNE 15TH 2017

From the mind of critic: "If all good things come to an end, do bad things come to an end? Is there an arbitrary time limit where if good or bad things go over, they're automatically finished? Is the time limit subjective, just like the idea of good and bad? Figuring out the world and what it means is a universal journey, even though it reveals different things for different people. Definitions of good and bad change depending on life experience, as well as education and upbringing. We can decipher solutions if we keep asking questions. Do good things have to end to make room for other good things, because we only have a finite amount of space? Can good and bad things introduce each other depending on our ignorance, apathy and complacency? If we hold onto something too long, the meaning changes. We must recognize it for the lessons and praise it has for us, and then let it go. If we want to stop the endless cycle of shit we're going through right now, we need to stop forcing life to happen how we think it should, and allow it to happen by letting it naturally evolve." ☺

FROM THE MIND OF CRITIC
JUNE 16TH 2017

From the mind of critic: "If coloring inside the lines makes a picture, does coloring outside the lines un-make a picture? Does drawing outside the lines create a new picture, bringing forth a sight we've never seen? Is this unknown creation, simply an instance of us creating our own reality? In art there are no mistakes, just constant adjustments and tweaks that evolve alongside our creative psyche. Same with life, there are no mistakes if we learn from them. Adjustments and tweaks aren't inherently bad just different, and can give us perspective we may have never known. Besides, who's drawing the lines and why, informs us of who's trying to control our behavior. Lines will always constrict our growth and dampen our creativity. Our collective mission is to feed creativity, not starve it." ☺

FROM THE MIND OF CRITIC
JUNE 17TH 2017

From the mind of critic: "If we're constantly searching for the fountain of youth, are we afraid of getting old? Are we scared we'll run out of time before we achieve our goals, so we attempt to add more time so we avoid ultimate regret? Do we feel we've wasted time with trivial pursuits? Do we need more time because after we achieve some goals, we realize there are many others? Time is a gift, not a curse. We only have a finite amount before it's over. We can spend time bettering our odds, by trying to look, think, act and feel younger. We can also spend time defying our odds, by going after our goals because it makes our heart sing, and because it's the right thing to do. We can spend all our time talking about the good old days, or we can plan our present so we have a better future. We can kill time, or we can spend time. We can't be complacent and enlightened, we have to choose." ☺

FROM THE MIND OF CRITIC

JUNE 20TH 2017

From the mind of critic: "If we measure twice and cut once, are we guaranteed a perfect cut? Will the cut be more neat and accurate, if a tape measure or straight edge is used to measure? Does it matter what brand of implement we use to measure, or just the experience, focus and integrity of the person doing the measuring? Preparation and action are completely symbiotic. One can't happen without the other. We could prepare all day long, putting all our time into deciding how to prepare, why we prepare, what we prepare and where. 90% of our energy is utilized organizing and outlining every detail, so when we sit down to do the actual thing, we're so tired from the prep, it feels like the work has already been done. Some things need more prep than others before action, and that's fine. We just can't brainwash ourselves into thinking prep is the work. We prep specifically so we can act, not to block us from doing so. We can measure twice, three times, hell even eight times, but if we never cut, there's no point in measuring."☺

FROM THE MIND OF CRITIC
JUNE 21ST 2017

From the mind of critic: "Do stereo-"types" matter, when looking for the most accurate representation of music? Does Sony, Bose or Panasonic amplify what music actually is, much more than cheaper brands? Does the stereo-"type" not matter, because although the music amplifies differently through different brands and devices, it's still music? Music will sound different coming from an RCA record player, compared to a Bose home theater system. Just like comments, ideas and experiences will sound different coming from a rich white guy in San Francisco, compared to a poor black man in Birmingham. Neither one is more credible, and neither's opinion is more accurate. However, we must listen to find out what's true, and what's false. Once we realize nobody's opinion about a certain group or ethnicity is 100% correct, because they haven't met every person from that group or ethnicity, we'll see stereotypes float away once we open our eyes and ears, and close our mouths. Stereotypes only exist, because people put their faith in them. If we stop putting our faith in them, they'll float away like American TV manufacturing." ☺

FROM THE MIND OF CRITIC

JUNE 22ND 2017

From the mind of critic: "If we make mountains out of mole hills, do we make mole hills out of mountains? Do we make small problems seem insurmountable, because we deem ourselves unworthy of success? Do we make huge problems seem insignificant, because we see them as not personally affecting us? Do we simply ignore everything, because we consciously believe ignorance is bliss? Some of us are drama magnets, while some of us are drama repellants. Sometimes our ego overshadows problems all the little people have, making us think we don't have those problems because we're better than them. Sometimes our self-esteem drops so low, we think we can't get past the simplest task, because positivity and happiness are meant for others. Once we realize that not blinding ourselves is the only way to truly see, we'll understand not making problems bigger than they are, and not thinking other people's issues can't happen to us, is how we truly unite. We have a lot of mountains and hills to get past. We'll have a much better chance of success, if we see what's in front of us." ☺

FROM THE MIND OF CRITIC
JUNE 23RD 2017

From the mind of critic: "If this country is built on united we stand and divided we fall, are we so concerned with being the person who does the uniting, that we're willing to divide until everyone comes to our side? Is our self-esteem so low that we're willing to destroy the world, just so we can rebuild it in our image? Have we never authentically stood up before, and are simply unfamiliar with the procedure? Believing in America isn't a bad thing, believing our version is better than somebody else's, is where we run into trouble. Once we realize uniting with others doesn't rob us of our beliefs, but adds to them, we'll see that whether we believe we have to divide before uniting, destroy before creating or war for peace, saying one thing and doing another is our biggest impediment to collective forward progress. We can stand together and unite, or we can fall together and divide, those are our only options." ☺

FROM THE MIND OF CRITIC

JUNE 24TH 2017

From the mind of critic: "If we have our cake and eat it too, isn't that the point? Isn't the idea of procuring cake, to eat it? If we have more cake than our neighbor, do we still attempt to take theirs, because we fear they're going to take ours? If we have mere crumbs, do we yearn for a slice of our own, because we've never been privileged enough to eat an entire untouched piece? What if the entire world is about getting cake, eating it and then getting more, but we happen to like pie? There's a reason avarice and pride are one of the seven deadly sins, and humility isn't. If we're afraid of losing a smidgen of what we have, to people who have but a fraction, we must ask why. Once we realize procuring wealth and building ourselves up is only detrimental when propelled by the destruction of others, we'll see being rich or poor isn't bad in and of itself, because our intent steers us in a positive or negative direction. We all like cake, we all think it's delicious, we just can't steal it from others, and not expect them to steal it from us." ☺

FROM THE MIND OF CRITIC
JUNE 27TH 2017

From the mind of critic: "If we're supposed to get truth from the writing on the wall, what do we do when the writing fades, corrodes and washes away? Do we trudge down to the store for writing implements, so we can restore our version of what the writing said? Do we rummage for implements we already have, so as to have no influence when we recreate exactly what the original writing conveyed? Did we disagree with the writing on the wall anyway, so not only do we fail to restore it, we cheer its funeral? Being perceptive enough to truly see what's in front of us, is one of the most important aspects of welcoming our positive evolution. Signs and messages come from everywhere, contain every point of view and change meanings depending on our perception. We can see them as helping or hurting, depending on the density of fog we're looking through. Once we realize the writing on the wall is a suggested diagram, not chiseled in stone, we'll see we can take it or leave it, just like the good and bad things in life. If we don't pay attention, we'll never receive the universe's guidance in moving our species forward. The writing on the wall might change, but like us, it simply evolves with the times." ☺

FROM THE MIND OF CRITIC

JUNE 28TH 2017

From the mind of critic: "If nothing quite goes with peanut butter like jelly, so much so that it's a cliché, what about peanut butter and honey? What about peanut butter and bacon, or god-forbid peanut butter and pickles? What about eating peanut butter hot, cold, smooth, nutty, on bread or a tortilla? We all have favorites, just like society has favorites they wish we would adopt as our own. Sometimes they coincide, and sometimes they don't. When favorites differ, is when we either buck the system, or revel in the status quo. We must never forget that our favorites, rebellious turning points and status quo will always differ from our neighbors because of unique life experience. Once we realize all these points of view don't discount our opinion, but add to the broadening of our horizons, we'll see what we've heard isn't always right, but if we don't listen, we won't have the material to decipher what right is. Peanut butter and jelly is a great thing, but if we never acknowledge the greatness of peanut butter and honey, we'll continue living under the false assumption that we're the center of the universe." ☺

FROM THE MIND OF CRITIC

JUNE 29TH 2017

From the mind of critic: "If our car needs gas to run, does it matter the octane? Can we actually tell if our car runs better with higher quality gas? Does one station offer higher quality fuel than another, making our drive smoother? Is that smoother drive an illusion, a peace of mind that our drive is easier, when it might be the opposite? Our bodies need fuel to run, just like our minds. Fueling up with high quality is always good, eating more natural foods and ingesting intellectual stimulation is never a bad thing. We go wrong when we think higher quality fuel, will guarantee an easier and smoother trip. We can get caught up with what we need to move forward and the way to move forward, instead of simply moving forward. Once we realize getting stuck on words, instead of the concept they describe prevents our positive evolution, we'll see that arguing over semantics will drive us all backwards. Our car needs fuel, but if we spend all our time arguing about octane, we'll never get where we need to go." ☺

FROM THE MIND OF CRITIC

JULY 1ST 2017

From the mind of critic: "If we're supposed to be emotionally and spiritually satisfied when we accomplish goals, how come we instantly see a million more things we want to do? Are we not giving ourselves credit for doing 100 things, because we have 1000 more to do? Does our self-esteem sag, because our puny goals don't compare to the grandiose accomplishments of our neighbor? Do new goals appear, specifically because previously achieved goals opened a door? Whether or not we believe there's no there there, doesn't make it any less true. Once we get where we want to go, we realize there are all these other places we want to go as well. Once we realize life really is a journey and not a destination, we'll see each conscious step forward we take brings us one step closer to enlightenment, by constantly absorbing and letting go. The more doors we walk through, the more doors appear. We can either continue to walk through them, or sit idly by and watch other people walk through them." ☺

FROM THE MIND OF CRITIC
JULY 4TH 2017

From the mind of critic: "When we drive into the sunset, is that the end? Are we glad our run is over, because misery is no longer? Are we sad we're at the end, because of unchecked boxes on our bucket list? Are we indifferent because of the zillion possibilities out there, which we couldn't possibly choose between? Is this sunset real, metaphorical, philosophical, political, religious or created in a lab? Whether we see a sunset at the end of our day, life, at the end of a test, trial or warranty, it represents finality. The measure of that finality is up to us. We could be sun setting on a stage in life, where we've learned lessons and moved on. We could be sun setting on an empire we've controlled for a long time, that's now crumbling because people are rising up. Sunsets, like life are what we make them. We just have to remember ending a run or a stage isn't inherently bad, it's only a test we have to pass to get where we need to go." ☺

FROM THE MIND OF CRITIC
JULY 5TH 2017

From the mind of critic: "If we're running a marathon, do we pace ourselves so we don't burn out early? Do we sprint as hard as we can, not thinking we'll burn out, only that we want to beat our opponents? Do we realize we're running a marathon, but have strategized for a much shorter race? Unless we want to severely shorten our windows of opportunity, we better prepare for life. Since we know our short time on this earth can be taken away at any time, we should never arbitrarily make it shorter. Difficulty comes when we try to balance quickly taking advantage of opportunities, and allowing tasks to be done the right way because we've given them the time they deserve. Life is a marathon, uniquely choreographed for each of us. We must find our goldilocks zone to succeed. Once we do, positive and conscious collective evolution is inevitable." ☺

FROM THE MIND OF CRITIC
JULY 6TH 2017

From the mind of critic: "If we have to do what we have to do, so we can do what we want to do, what do we have to do? Do we all need to do the same things, because we all want the same things? Are we implored to do something different, because our wants are unique by virtue of being human? Do we all have the same basic needs, but different wants depending on our background? In a nutshell, humans have the same basic needs and wants, with additional unique needs and wants based on environment, culture and upbringing. To know the difference between "unique" and "basic", we must figure out what we want. This can be difficult, but becomes easier with practice. Once we realize our needs and wants evolve as we evolve, we'll see none of us know what we truly want, but the more we vigilantly ask tough questions, our needs and wants won't be in conflict, they'll be symbiotic. We can't know what we want, without knowing what we need. If we don't know what we need, how can we know what others need? How can we know somebody without knowing ourselves?" ☺

FROM THE MIND OF CRITIC

JULY 7TH 2017

From the mind of critic: "If we spread a puzzle on the table, and see where half of it fits together, does it instantly become less enjoyable? Is it more fun to have a head start, before it becomes boring due to its increasing easiness? Are puzzles never enjoyable because they're too hard, so we wait for somebody else to put them together? Life features few events which easily fit together in a simple to understand picture. Life can also have many events, which fit together easily, but take considerably longer to decipher. Once we realize events in life are always interconnected no matter how disconnected they seem, we'll see life grows chaotically complex when we try to instantly snap it together. Life gets easier when we pick an area to start from, and go from there. Some puzzles might be hard, but if we don't look at all the pieces, we'll never figure out how they fit." ☺

FROM THE MIND OF CRITIC
JULY 8TH 2017

From the mind of critic: "If money is speech what's louder, passion or dollars? Are there passionate billionaires who want to save the environment, and help humans consciously evolve? Are there passionate hundred-aires who want to save the economy, and logically prove that if billionaires paid income taxes equal to workers, free college and free healthcare wouldn't even be a question? Do we value free speech more if it emanates from a stock portfolio or hedge fund, rather than a union or paycheck earner? Citizens United solidified what has been tradition for millennia, that the rich are seen as more credible than the poor. That somebody who collects dividend checks should be taken more seriously than somebody who collects paychecks. Passion is a human feeling which affects all of us who are human. Once we realize some passion tries to drown out other passion with dollars, we'll see the further we get away from the actual issue at hand, the easier our thoughts will be steered with money. Speech comes out of our minds through our mouths, and money is something physical we hold in our hands. We all deserve to be heard, and we all want to make change. Until money ejects out of our minds through our mouths, speech and money will never be equal." ☺

FROM THE MIND OF CRITIC
JULY 11TH 2017

From the mind of critic: "Since lines are utilized to keep order, and we purposely go outside the lines, are we sowing disorder? If we blur lines, is it compromise because we're only going half as far as we could be? If we're unsatisfied with the lines society has set, does blurring them have the same effect, which is to sow confusion? Are lines an arbitrary means of control meant for people to internalize, so they don't fight back, and begin living the creed, "it is what it is?" The idea of lines are objective, the people who formulate, design and implement them are subjective. Powerful and influential people crave more power and influence once they get their first taste. Drug addicts always want more drugs, just like business and political leaders always want more power. This act of chasing the dragon is what causes lines to be designed, so a steady stream of supply keeps flowing. Once we realize lines only have control over us because we put our faith in them, we'll see that the more we decipher life with critical thought, the less we'll need lines at all. Lines will show us the control we're all under, if we open our eyes." ☺

FROM THE MIND OF CRITIC
JULY 12TH 2017

From the mind of critic: "When swimming in a cold river, do we start by dipping our toes to test the temperature? Do we walk in slowly till the water hits our thighs, deciding whether to jump in or not? Do we feel how cold the water is from the moment it touches our skin? Do we know that if we're ever going to swim, we have to say screw being uncomfortable in the short run, so we can end up being comfortable in the long run? Life can be dark and cold, where all hopes and dreams get swallowed up by the necessity to survive. Life can also be a light and warm place, where all hopes and dreams get lifted up by the necessity to survive. Our perception determines the darkness of life. We must remember darkness doesn't have to be scary, only unknown. Once we realize the results of moving forward are always unknown beforehand, we'll see our speed of entering life's journey is based on our passion for enjoying how good life can be. The water is always cold before we enter, the length of time the coldness sticks around, is based on our willingness to swim." ☺

FROM THE MIND OF CRITIC

JULY 13TH 2017

From the mind of critic: "If we all know one of the biggest problems we have with garbage is packaging materials, how come we keep buying products specifically because of the packaging? Is it bright colors, celebrity endorsements or alleged health benefits that pull us in, regardless of what's actually in the box? Are we afraid to buy products that don't look fancy but work better, because we don't want to be seen using them? We all flock to bright colors and flashing lights because we're human, and they attract our gaze. Whether its people, places, events or interactions, if we're so enamored with physical appearance, hype and rhetoric that truth flies out the window, we'll erect the worst kind of phony filler to keep us satiated. For truth in advertising to be effective, we can't glaze over when it comes time to ask critical questions. Being distracted, duped and gullible are reactions we have complete control over, once we slow down to comprehend the reality on the ground. The volume of packaging materials goes up when we're complacent and apathetic, and goes down when we're conscious and kind. We're implored to ask which way will help us collectively evolve." ☺

FROM THE MIND OF CRITIC
JULY 14TH 2017

From the mind of critic: "If we all love to party, how come we insist on partying with like-minded people? Do we think we party better than those other people, because they don't know how to have fun? Do the drinks we have, the food we eat and the games we play ooze more authenticity from our pinkie, than those other party people have in their whole bodies? Do we comprehend the evolutionary importance of partying with people we don't agree with? Being a Democrat is not better than being a Republican, is not better than being a Green, a Libertarian etc. If the only reason we're a party member is to raise money, or to gain support from ingrained swamp rats, then we are the problem. Gaining an advantage over our opponent is normal, selling our soul and stepping on necks to be successful is not. Once we realize we all want our voices heard, we'll see no voice is more important than another, if we still want to live in a Democracy. Partying together is always better than partying separate. When we achieve unity, we won't need to set up parties, because it'll be just how life operates." ☺

FROM THE MIND OF CRITIC

JULY 15TH 2017

From the mind of critic: "If placing blame for our indiscretions is how we sleep at night, are we trying to hide ourselves, from ourselves? Are we scared to be honest, because we'd have to endure short term pain and anguish? Does the idea of being uncomfortable for even a second, feel like the worst pain in the world? Do we put this pain onto others when blaming them, while also comforting them so we can play both sides? Accountability is something many people preach, but few practice. We all want others to be straight shooters, and not beat around the bush when expressing what they think. We then cut them down by saying their opinions are inaccurate, and aren't representative of rational human thought. Once we realize when we project ignorance unto others, we're forcing them to picture themselves as negatively as we picture ourselves, we'll see scapegoating never solves anything, because it creates the cliché of kicking the can down the road. Placing blame moves us backward, while accepting responsibility moves us forward. When making our directional choice, we must remember that united we stand, and divided we fall." ☺

FROM THE MIND OF CRITIC
JULY 18TH 2017

From the mind of critic: "Is the amount of time it takes for dust to settle, equal to the amount we kick up? Does the speed or power of our kick, make the dust settle slower? Does the determined nature of our constant and repeated dust kicking, cause dust to permanently emulsify with the air? Does our fear of dirt keep us from collectively evolving? We all must get our hands dirty from time to time, because change is inevitable. Not being satisfied with the status quo no matter how generationally ingrained, blueprints where dust needs to be roiled. We run into problems when we know dust needs to be kicked up, but leave it to somebody else, because we think our legs aren't strong enough. Once we realize inaction and non-purposeful action are enemies of a free society, we'll see real change happens with authentic first steps. Kicking up dust can change the world, as long as we remember it eventually settles back down." ☺

FROM THE MIND OF CRITIC

JULY 19TH 2017

From the mind of critic: "If we're in an epic battle to balance what's probable with what's possible, how do we set achievable goals? Do we shoot for the moon, knowing possibilities abound when we consciously journey forward? Do we stay reserved, knowing things are only probable when we start at the beginning and work forward, instead of at the end working backward? Do we stay balanced, because we know goals are only achievable when we don't get in our own way? Some of us are more left brained, and some more right brained. However, if we don't use our whole brain, we're not using it at all. If critical thinking demands we objectively observe what's in front of us, then our decisions must be based on our heart and mind, not either or. Once we realize to discover what's probable we must analyze what's possible, we'll see looking at options, means expecting new information to suddenly appear. Researching and dreaming make us complete human beings. We achieve balance when probabilities and possibilities merge, revealing their symbiotic relationship with our heart and soul." ☺

FROM THE MIND OF CRITIC

JULY 20TH 2017

From the mind of critic: : "If what doesn't kill us makes us stronger, do world record weight lifters have to endure immense persecution, racism, hate, violence, ethnic cleansing or disasters specifically so they can break records? Do we become strong, by overcoming what we didn't think we could? Do we become weak, by staying neutral when we knew we could act? Do we become enlightened, by taking everything on a case by case basis? We all have adversity to overcome, obstacles to get past and goals to achieve. Gaining life experience through testing our mettle is how we build character. That creation will serve us throughout our lives, defining who we are, and how we view the world. Can we become strong human beings without going through hardship, sure, but it's rare. Once we realize rules can be exceptions, and exceptions can be norms, we'll see unless we're open to life's entirety, discernment will disappear, and we'll be helpless against the whims of whichever way the wind blows. When we figure out strength isn't always physical, our perceptions begin to benefit our soul." ☺

FROM THE MIND OF CRITIC

JULY 21ST 2017

From the mind of critic: "If the whole is only equal to the sum of its parts, how can we not sweat the small stuff? If we're supposed to pay attention to the bigger picture, how can we if we neglect everything which makes up that bigger picture? Do we hang on to all of life's little moments, hoping they'll never end out of fear they'll never return? Does the tightness of our grip, change a moment's inherent meaning? We've all heard the cliché don't sweat the small stuff, that to succeed in life we have to pay attention to the bigger picture. The keyword in that phrase isn't small stuff, its sweat. Taking it a step further, we shouldn't sweat the bigger picture either. Once we realize being in the moment, means enjoying or dreading moments for what they are by seeing how they're interconnected, we'll understand life as a constant letting go process. We as humans become equal to the sum of our parts, when consciousness flows through us with the power of our determined soul." ☺

FROM THE MIND OF CRITIC
JULY 29TH 2017

From the mind of critic: If we all attest to the benefits unions have fought for over the years, how come we allow our voices to be silenced, by letting unions get demonized? Was fighting for workers' rights like the moon landing, where we made this great accomplishment a few times, figured it was good enough, and moved on to bigger and better things? Was our will weaker than the business leaders who waited out the battle, because they knew sooner or later we'd have to pay bills? After a few victories did we become complacent and apathetic, helping the union busters chip away, until our victories were barely recognizable? Without unions and the bloody and violent battles of our parents and grandparents, we wouldn't have weekends off, paid sick days, maternity leave, bereavement leave, overtime pay, holiday pay, child labor laws, and a plethora of product and workplace safety regulations. If we don't care about those things, that's our right as Americans, and we don't have to support unions. However, if we care one iota about being treated like a human being in the workplace, we must keep our voice strong. We must sustain our fight as long as it takes, so we all get what we deserve. Because if we think businesses will give us benefits we deserve out of the goodness of their hearts, there's some ocean front property in Arizona we'd be interested in.

If unions consist of our voices, but are painted as evil, are we going to let ourselves be labeled evil, or are we going to stand up?" ☺

FROM THE MIND OF CRITIC AUGUST 1ST 2017

From the mind of critic: "If we fly through life by the seat of our pants, while knowing it's the definition of adventure, is it any surprise they call life an adventure? Did we think life would be easy or hard because of who came before us? Do we get so overwhelmed by the chaos of life, that the only thing we can do is fly by the seat of our pants, therefore expecting adventure? They say we should expect the unexpected, so we aren't caught flat footed. If we want to get the most out of life, we must be kind to ourselves, by taking advantage of every opportunity which builds us up, leaving behind every one which tears us down. Flying by the seat of our pants might be uncomfortable, but as long as our heart and mind are headed in a positive and evolutionary direction, we'll be just fine. If we do what we need, so we can do what we want, it'll clear our conscious and clean our soul." ☺

FROM THE MIND OF CRITIC AUGUST 2ND 2017

From the mind of critic: "If we see smoke but can't find the gun, will we forever chase our tail? Do we question our sanity, worldview, perceptions and choices if the smoke hitting us in the face gets thicker and thicker, with nary a gun to be found? Do we plow through the smoke, because we know the more it billows, the stronger the fire? We all know the phrase, "there's what we know to be true, and what we can prove in court". When we know things are true because we witnessed them, and which spawn numerous antidotes, we start believing in truth. Signs, symbols and leads appear, because our perception is colored, and our mission focused. If we don't find answers soon enough, we can't give up. Not every wild goose chase ends with a big payoff. However, if something is hidden from public view, those orchestrating the cover up will distract us with whatever they can conjure. They'll stop at nothing to make us hit dead ends. If we happen to bust through, they'll make us believe we're insane; maybe that's their real power. Whether or not we find the smoking gun or the fire is beside the point. We can't let the bad actors in this world crush our goodness. We spread light to others, when we get them to believe in their own." ☺

FROM THE MIND OF CRITIC AUGUST 3RD 2017

From the mind of critic: "Does everything have to be uncomfortable, before it's comfortable? Do we have to endure enormous hardships, specifically so we don't take good times for granted? Are we forced to learn lessons we've been escaping for years, because they've become infinitely more vibrant because we've escaped them? Must we realize we aren't the best and don't know everything, specifically to help others discover the same concept? Whether it's old vs. young, man vs. woman, liberal vs, conservative or any other arbitrary battle, we all must endure a changing and evolving world if we want to accomplish something meaningful. Once we realize we're all struggling to leave a positive mark, we'll see it's the common thread which holds us together as humans. We can't shy away from challenges, because there's always light on the other side. If something is easily moving us forward, we don't have to purposely make it harder, just to convince ourselves we're deserving; consciously building one more collective human roadblock. Turning self-sabotage into motivation is hard, but becomes easier when we open our eyes to the beauty of the world." ☺

FROM THE MIND OF CRITIC AUGUST 4TH 2017

From the mind of critic: "If we get upset politicians are doing crazy things, do we get upset at ourselves for the same reason? If we see our President, Senator, Congressman, County Supervisor, Mayor or city councilman circumventing the law to serve their own interests, are we doing the same thing? If we hate politicians but love our person, are we subconsciously admitting we don't care about anybody not in our circle? One of the biggest things we can do as humans to further evolution, is realizing we're not the center of the universe. This self-imposed roadblock grows exponentially when we reach elected office, because of self-aggrandizement. All the self-loathing, low self-esteem and pissing contests we endure as civilians, become magnified when we realize we have no control over our neighbors. We start cutting others down to build ourselves up, heading in the opposite direction of what all men are created equal is supposed to mean. To fix our politics, we must fix ourselves. To do that, we can't be afraid to wave at a stranger walking down the street. They might be the person meant to guide us in the positive direction we've been searching for." ☺

FROM THE MIND OF CRITIC AUGUST 8TH 2017

From the mind of critic: "If we learned long ago that we're unique snowflakes, why do we get mad at others for being different? Do we not see the correlation between the size, design, weight, temperature and elevation of snowflakes, and the height, weight, gender, sexual orientation, religion, skin color, traditions, age and intelligence of humans? Do we see how snowflakes and human intelligence are unique, but have never put 2 and 2 together? If we create our own reality, then our perceptions do the creating. When we understand a concept, it's hard to link it, if we've never found commonality before. Practice doesn't make perfect. We can't be perfect because we're not robots, practice makes better. If we understand something is unique, we can't get mad at somebody for proving something we already understood. We must comprehend that we're all unique, and all the same. We're unique by virtue of being human, and we're the same for the same reason."☺

FROM THE MIND OF CRITIC AUGUST 9TH 2017

From the mind of critic: "If we can be all we can be in the Army, is it the only way we can be all we can be? Does it instill that we're not good enough, and can't possibly enhance our personal, spiritual, physical and mental selves as good as the Army can? Do we believe the Army knows us better than we know ourselves? Can an outside organization remove the roadblocks we've set in place of our positive forward progress? No matter the color of our skin, the size of our bank account, the language we speak or who we choose to love, we're all looking for happiness, and to make sense out of chaos. We do that by learning who we are, what we want and what motivates us to get there. We can change ourselves, because only we truly know ourselves. If somebody says we can only reach our true potential through them, they're praying on our reliance on instant gratification. The Army might be able to make us all we can be, but so can literally anything else depending on our perception. We must not be afraid of hard work now, to have a joyful soul later. We become better, only when we allow ourselves to be better." ☺

FROM THE MIND OF CRITIC AUGUST 10TH 2017

From the mind of critic: "When we see nothing but darkness, do we expect light around every corner? When we see nothing but light, do we expect darkness around every corner? Do we expect the worse, so we don't get let down? Do we expect things to turn out, so we don't have to put in any work? Are we afraid to put ourselves out there, whether it's negatively or positively? The first step in our journey is difficult, but it's the most important. Once we put that first foot forward, everything opens up. We'll witness a lot of light, dark and everything in between as our experience is added to, and perceptions adjust. We may have several consecutive bad experiences, convincing us nothing good will ever happen. We might have several consecutive good experiences, convincing us nothing bad will ever happen. This whole process started with expecting the unexpected, but also got road blocked because we expected the unexpected. We can't get so set in our ways we think nothing will change. Light and dark are balances, not constants. Balance is about accepting change, and constants are about accepting stagnation. Do we want balance to help us reach the light, or stagnation to help us reach the dark? When we feel gratitude for what is, the answer appears." ☺

FROM THE MIND OF CRITIC AUGUST 11TH 2017

From the mind of critic: "If change doesn't happen unless we rock the boat, do we get seasick? Does rocking the boat make us nauseous? Does doing nothing allow us to ride the same old calm seas? Do we have to see how bad things can get, before they improve so we see how good they can get? The amount of boat rocking needed, is equal to the size of change needed. While the size of change is subjective, we must always be prepared to be uncomfortable in the short run, so we can be comfortable in the long run. This is the essence of gratitude. We use what we have to strive for more. Once we realize rocking the boat will make somebody sick, we'll see once consciousness, humanism and accountability are accounted for, we won't be the ones hanging over the side. Remembering why we rock the boat is nature's Dramamine." ☺

FROM THE MIND OF CRITIC
AUGUST 12TH 2017

From the mind of critic: "If life speeds by so quickly when we're older that years melt together, and life crawls so slowly when we're younger that years seem like centuries, is it ever possible to find common ground? Is the definition of balancing fast and slow, simply called living in the moment? Whether we have lots of memories because we're old, or are planning for them because we're young, we must be conscious of what's in front of our face. We stay conscious by feeling gratitude for everything we have, helping us feel and utilize each and every moment. Once our energy is raised, we're motivated to become the most loving, peaceful and fulfilled human being we could possibly be. The idea is not to always look forward or always look back, but to simply look. Whether we're old or young and want to slow down or speed up, the more we build memories now, the closer our goldilocks zone becomes." ☺

FROM THE MIND OF CRITIC AUGUST 15TH 2017

From the mind of critic: "When answers to deep seeded problems only spawn more questions, are we discouraged to keep asking? If the light at the end of the tunnel is the furthest point on the horizon, but doesn't become closer the more steps we take, are we discouraged from moving forward? If the darkness is getting darker, is it because of fear that light is taking over? The sure sign of knowledge is that there's a lot left to learn. Just because we don't know why racist Nazi scum are emboldened to walk down the street with assault rifles, in a self-proclaimed action to carry out Trump's agenda, doesn't mean we don't ask why. Once we identify the right questions, we'll realize we might have known the answer all along, but were afraid to admit it. This personal fear over ugliness we've always known, overpowered our love, humanism, accountability and critical thinking that could've not only prevented this current pot of hate from boiling over, but could've shrunk it into a corner years ago. Questions might only lead to more questions, but if we stop asking, darkness will seize control. We fight hate and darkness, by standing with love and light, and keep standing until the entire world is engulfed." ☺

FROM THE MIND OF CRITIC AUGUST 16TH 2017

From the mind of critic: "If hate and racism are caused by ignorance, how do we get some to realize they might not know everything? How do we stop the cycle of ignorance, to apathy, to complacency, to hate and back to ignorance? How do we realize we might not be the perfect human specimen we portray ourselves to be? You'd think it wouldn't be hard in the 21st century to say Nazis, White Nationalists, White Supremacists, Neo Nazis, Peckerwoods and 1 percenters are not only detrimental, but are an extremely dark and violent effort to destroy what America is supposed to be. Since we're currently in that stage, we must recognize it, and not beat around the bush. To recognize our current predicament, we have to talk openly and honestly. Once we're used to talking humanely and peacefully, we'll see ignorance float away. This disappearing act happens because the people we've been racist and hateful to, are enduring the same struggles as we are. Once poor Whites, Blacks, Hispanics, Asians and Native Americans see they're going through the same hardships, they'll unite. Isn't unification what we're looking for, recognizing we're different and the same, at the same time? Isn't that how we beat back hate and ignorance?" ☺

FROM THE MIND OF CRITIC AUGUST 17TH 2017

From the mind of critic: "If bread and circuses weld us into survival mode, can humanism and accountability melt through? Is the person we trust to cure societal blindness, the same person who welded in bread and circuses? Do outside forces convince us cures are fake, because they have a great chance of success? Success is a subjective term like love, hate, joy and sadness. This doesn't mean success isn't real, it means only we determine when something is for our personal and collective uplift. Control of the powerless by the powerful, has been levied ever since humans started walking upright. The apathy and complacency which allows us to live our life and make the best of a bad situation, is exactly what cements our role of being controlled. We destroy this cycle by standing up, speaking out and loving our fellow humans like our species depends on it, because the vampires at the top never get enough blood. We break bread and circuses, by actually breaking bread with our neighbors, and realizing how much of a circus our life has become." ☺

FROM THE MIND OF CRITIC AUGUST 18TH 2017

From the mind of critic: If we arrived into the world with directions, would they be easy to follow? Would the first ten be the most important, like the Bill of Rights? Are the rules in an arbitrary order, and like life, we take what works, and leave what doesn't? Babies don't come out of the womb with toe tag instructions, any more than adults burst into adulthood with a guaranteed plan to move forward. Life is hard work, especially when deciphering how to make our hopes and dreams reality. Life is much more fulfilling when we figure out how to get past obstacles ourselves, as opposed to a unisex, androgynous, generic, robotic and systematic one size fits all plan to be a joyful and satisfied person. Are we looking for somebody to do all the thinking and strategic planning, so adversity, hardship and character building trials and tribulations are dealt with by somebody else? If we're not looking for the easy way out, and know the importance of our soul's development, we'll not only heed advice, but will blaze our own trail. "If all else fails read the directions" works, if we're putting together a table, but not for putting together a joyful, peaceful and fulfilling life. That we have to figure out for ourselves." ☺

FROM THE MIND OF CRITIC AUGUST 19TH 2017

From the mind of critic: "Do we kill violence with violence, or do we kill peace with violence? Do we kill peace with peace, or do we kill violence with peace? Do we even know why we get mad at somebody for being different? We can rage instantly, or it can slowly build. If our only reason for anger is that a group of people are taking everything from us, when "that group" had everything taken from them, by those taking from us all, then we have gullibility to blame for our high blood pressure. Violence breeds violence, and peace breeds peace. Whether it's a single person, a group, a rally or a march, we kill violence and peace by doing the opposite. It might take a lot of peace to squash violence that doesn't want to relinquish power after hundreds of years, but a lot of peace can be awoken. We just have to ask if we we're willing to show up in massive enough numbers, so peace is fully displayed." ☺

FROM THE MIND OF CRITIC AUGUST 22ND 2017

From the mind of critic: "If a solar eclipse blocks our view of the sun, and foggy skies block our view of the eclipse, did the force blocking the sun, get blocked out itself? Is it simply two different methods of blocking the sun, depriving us of vitamin D? Are there infinite methods for blocking the sun? Do our eyes receive the blocking method corresponding with our perspective and life experience? The sun is always there no matter what blocks it, because if it disappeared, so would life. It's the same concept with light and darkness in our soul. We must do what we can to let our light shine, knowing outside entities will do what they can to block our illumination. Sometimes we can stop them, sometimes we can't, and sometimes our light is shining whether we know it to or not. Once we realize blocking something from blotting out our light is still blocking light, we'll see if our light is blocked from view, we need to build a tunnel or bridge, not more walls. An eclipse might block our sun, but if we don't learn lessons from the darkness, light could disappear forever. Don't block light, allow it to absorb." ☺

FROM THE MIND OF CRITIC AUGUST 23RD 2017

From the mind of critic: "Is our ladder to success laid out when we start our journey, or are steps added as we move forward? If our ladder is waiting for us, with pre-designed steps toward a pre-determined outcome, who does the determining and what's their motivation? If the skeleton of our ladder is waiting without steps, and pointed toward the unknown, how do we build steps and ensure their authenticity? We all have the opportunity to journey down infinite paths, headed in infinite directions. Sometimes these paths have step by step instructions. Sometimes they have instructions in no particular order. Sometimes there aren't instructions at all, but signs and symbols which direct us to write our own instructions. Most of the time, not only are there no directions, but there's no visible path. Once we realize the unknown isn't scary, but new and intriguing, we'll see we create our own paths to success, by coming up with concrete steps that aren't pre-formulated or focus grouped. Stepladders are scary when we build steps as we climb, but are much sturdier in the long run." ☺

FROM THE MIND OF CRITIC AUGUST 25TH 2017

From the mind of critic: "When we're frayed to the edges, and a million people want a million things from us yesterday, do we choose not to act, in interest of slowing our out of control mind? Do we attempt everything, knowing we can't accomplish it all, then get sad and depressed when we prove ourselves right? Do we choose what builds us up, and leave everything else behind as unsolicited hot air? If there's one thing we don't need more of in this day and age, it's more hot air. The created climate of Trump and all matter of darkness is in great abundance, fraying us to our core. Once we realize our core is the deepest part of who we are, as opposed to who we claim to be, we'll see the more we know ourselves, what we want, what mark we want to leave, and the kindness and gratitude to get us there, the less anybody will fray us, no matter the temperature or velocity of their hot air. We can't ever do what a million people say. Will we choose to stay the same, or move forward?" ☺

FROM THE MIND OF CRITIC AUGUST 26TH 2017

From the mind of critic: "If stereotypes are based on false assumptions, do those false assumptions cause the ignorant vitriol plaguing our politics? Is every member of a certain group all one way or all another, never deviating from a pre-meditated plan for how a race, culture or religion can be controlled? Are we all unique snowflakes, but get jealous of others who seem more successful, more content, and are taking everything from us in their climb to the top? None of us know everything in the world, nor could our delicate minds contain everything anyway. When we don't know something or somebody, we could get scared and feel less than because of ingrained messages we've been told all our lives. As humans, we want to be as comfortable as possible. Once we realize comfort isn't achieved when others feel discomfort, but only when we all feel comfort, we'll see stereotypes only fuel division in our species, and the crumbs elites allow us to have. How about we unite, and decide what few crumbs we'll allow the elites to have? How about we stop fighting each other, and stand up against a system that's keeping us all down?" ☺

FROM THE MIND OF CRITIC AUGUST 29TH 2017

From the mind of critic: "Whether we drew inside the lines or not, what color crayons did we grab as a kid from that big box of 64? Did the color we grabbed, determine whether we colored inside the lines or not? Did we walk up to the box already knowing the color we wanted, because we've been told for generations only one color is the right color? Did we know our color choice, only because we knew what picture we wanted to create? Do shades differ from brand to brand? Are certain colors made for inside the lines and some for the outside, or is that what some people want us to think? We can choose to draw inside the lines or outside the lines, and with or without color. Once we realize color makes every picture beautiful, we'll see it's not the color that matters, but the picture itself. Humans and crayons may not have much in common, but the more color we have, the more beauty life reveals. How boring would life be in only one color? We don't live in a black and white world, but one that's rainbow." ☺

FROM THE MIND OF CRITIC AUGUST 30TH 2017

From the mind of critic: "If we all band together during a natural disaster, regardless of previous biases, why does it die off after the initial response? Do we feel the disaster got us out of a spiteful, vitriolic and divisive routine, but now that the initial shock is over, we must get back to our normal lives, which include a vitriolic, spiteful and divisive routine? Do we get stuck in hyper-survival mode, where we help somebody, because we know that 10 minutes later, they could be saving our life? Whether natural, political, financial, or lab or focus group created, disasters can be a great unifier. When all the chips are down, our humanity returns, otherwise the emotional disaster would take us all down. Once we realize some people's chips are down whether there's a disaster or not, we'll see if we observe signs and symbols of people hurting, before 130 mph winds and 50 inches of rain arrive, we wouldn't need a disaster to rekindle our humanity. Animosity, ignorance, jealousy, spitefulness and hate disappear when helping others, specifically because we're helping ourselves." ☺

FROM THE MIND OF CRITIC AUGUST 31ST 2017

From the mind of critic: "If darkness and dense fog covers our road ahead, how do we move forward? Do we go balls to the wall, plowing forward at breakneck speed without regard for safety? Does the fog make us choose a different route, but since it's hindering all routes, we stay stagnant? Is there a middle ground, where we move forward strategically, so we get where we want to go, but don't hurt ourselves or others in the process? The 24-7 365 deluge of mis-information we endure, can fog over any path we choose; the key word being CAN. Once we realize our critically thinking mind and kind loving soul are our fog lights, we'll see no matter how dense the fog, we can always move forward, if we choose to move forward. Fog only exists as an impediment, if we allow it to obscure our humanity." ☺

FROM THE MIND OF CRITIC SEPTEMBER 1ST 2017

From the mind of critic: "If we're all just links in the chain, if we're all just dust in the wind, if we're all just bricks in the wall, does anything we do matter? If we dislodge ourselves from the chain, wind and wall, does it affect structural integrity? Do links, bricks and dust simply get replaced if missing, or if they prove elusive, does major restructuring occur? Some of us may think one person can't change the world, but enough "one persons" can. Once we realize if people stopped believing in the prevailing wisdom, and stood up to make positive and conscious change, we'll discover we might actually get off our asses and do something. We might only be links, dust and bricks, but without our support, the chain, wind and wall wouldn't exist." ☺

FROM THE MIND OF CRITIC SEPTEMBER 2ND 2017

From the mind of critic: "If we've boiled down what we want to three things, do we organize our routine to achieve those three things? Is our life easier, because we know where to steer our actions? Is our life harder, because we only want to go after our three things, neglecting everything else? Can we find a happy medium, where going after our three things doesn't make us neglect anything, but enhances what's worth our time? Many of us struggle to discover what we're passionate about, that when we finally do, we're so exhausted we stay static. Discovery is only the first step, then comes planning and action. Once we realize the true meaning of "life is a journey", means we set our sights on what we want, then consciously move forward, we'll see we can achieve our goals by enjoying our journey, not by wearing blinders. We might really want success, to leave a mark and to find love, but the only thing we can guarantee is failure, if we don't utilize conscious effort. Is there anything we could be more grateful for, then discovering and then going after what makes our soul sing?" ☺

FROM THE MIND OF CRITIC SEPTEMBER 5TH 2017

From the mind of critic: "If we're consciously and confidently journeying toward enlightenment, but take a few side trails toward darkness, how do we find our way back? Do we remember we started in darkness, and left it behind by entering the light? Do we feel like since we blew it, we might as well really blow it, and make the darkness our permanent home? We all stray from our path from time to time, it's a very human thing to not be perfect. Once we realize no matter how much light (friends, family, love gratitude) surrounds us, darkness (sabotage, self-doubt, ignorance, self-pity and chasing the dragon of fleeting happiness) will always be there, we'll see the more we defend against darkness with love and gratitude, the shorter our turnaround time will be. Blinders aren't a cure for getting side tracked, love and gratitude are, which we can access anytime." ☺

FROM THE MIND OF CRITIC SEPTEMBER 6TH 2017

From the mind of critic: "If we've learned the lesson of being grateful for what we have, and not waiting till it's gone, is it still taken away? Do lessons keep repeating themselves until we've evolved past learning, and integrate them into our normal routine? If these lessons keep slapping us in the face, do we ask why us, or what now? With Harvey, and now Irma, we might be asking why these increasingly powerful storms, are happening with more frequency. The answer lies somewhere between the difference of wondering why, and asking why. When we start asking why, causes begin to emerge. Once we realize causes are easy to decipher when politics are deleted from the equation, and replaced by humanity, we'll see we learn lessons by consciously taking action the lessons specifically illuminated. Learning lessons are the first step, making an action plan is the next. Lessons stop smacking us in the face, when we stop letting fear and ignorance fog over our humanity." ☺

FROM THE MIND OF CRITIC SEPTEMBER 8TH 2017

From the mind of critic: "If two paths meet, do they intersect, or are they like strangers passing in the night? Do paths inherently change due to environment and politics, let alone other paths influencing its direction and purpose? Do paths contain blinders by moving at the same speed, and in the same direction no matter the stimuli? Do paths guide themselves, or do people traveling them determine their destiny? The paths we travel zig-zag, fork, parallel, detour, influence and are influenced, and that's only the paths within our journey. Once we realize seven billion people travel multiple paths as well, we'll see our paths always intersect and influence others, and vice versa. We influence and get influenced, that's just how the world works. The more we pay attention, the more control we have. The more control we have, the more we realize we can't control everything, only our reactions. As long as we keep the good and leave the bad, it won't matter how often our paths cross. In fact, the more our paths meet, the more opportunities we'll have to build each other up. Isn't that the point of everything?" ☺

FROM THE MIND OF CRITIC SEPTEMBER 12TH 2017

From the mind of critic: "If we wave at random strangers walking down the street, do we have a hidden agenda? Do we wave at some, while avoiding eye contact with others? Are we waving at our fellow humans, because they're journeying, just like we're journeying? Do we wave because it's a direct and personal interaction we can initiate, in an increasingly impersonal world? Do we wave simply because our parents and grandparents taught us to be neighborly? If we've ever been fishing or on a boat, we've waved at strangers whether we remember or not. It's friendly, neighborly, human, and a way to signal we're here, you're there, and we can help each other if need be. Once we realize waving at other fisherman or boaters, is like waving in regular life and for the same reason, we'll see the more we wave at fellow humans, the more human we become. Personal interactions are the little things which make life worth living. Sometimes when we wave people ignore, don't acknowledge, wave back, and sometimes they smile back. Isn't somebody we don't know making us randomly smile, while we make them randomly smile, the solution to most of the world's problems?" ☺

FROM THE MIND OF CRITIC SEPTEMBER 13TH 2017

From the mind of critic: "Do politics make us forget disasters, or do disasters make us forget politics? Does the permanent campaign get interrupted by mass devastation, or does a flood of humanity overtake ego in the eye of a category five? Does money overshadow critical thinking, or does critical thinking question the need for money? The ongoing debate of whether having nothing or everything shows true character, will rage until we allow our humanity to remain after a disaster subsides. What makes the determination difficult, is deciphering whether political rhetoric is genuine, or staged when destruction and tragedy hits. Is there a way to discuss the symptoms of a disease, and what led to a stage four prognosis so future cases can be prevented, without taking away from human suffering? Once we realize people listen to others talking to them, but not at them, we'll see polarization of disaster and tragedy only happen when humanity is removed. There will always be somebody who says we're politicizing, no matter what we do. If we don't feel comfortable discussing root causes while a disaster or tragedy is playing out, but insist on waiting till some arbitrary point down the line, we must ask ourselves, do we want to prevent tragedy, or feed tragedy? Solutions are only digestible when issues are fresh, not after they've gone stale." ☺

FROM THE MIND OF CRITIC SEPTEMBER 14TH 2017

From the mind of critic: "When a fellow human traveler bumps into us on the street and asks us what time it is, is it because they don't know, or because they do, but want our opinion? Can we deduce time without a clock or watch, but by whichever way the wind blows? Even if we know exactly and without a doubt what time it is, does human evolution require us to constantly check the time, because time was designed to keep rolling? One of the challenges of growing up on planet earth, is the knowledge that time is always moving. We can't stop it or slow it, we can only roll with it, or get left behind. Once we realize time is always progressing, whether it's man made numbers, or the constantly shifting sands of the prevailing wisdom, we'll see that time changes from moment to moment, culture to culture, government to government and person to person. If everybody has a different opinion of what time it is, how will we ever tell the time? Looking for "the time" is like chasing the dragon, we'll never catch it because it doesn't exist. Isn't our time better spent finding something which does exist like, "our time"? If we don't know "our time", how could we inform somebody of "their time", that's what we should be asking." ☺

FROM THE MIND OF CRITIC SEPTEMBER 16TH 2017

From the mind of critic: "If we float whichever way the wind blows, we seemingly have no control, but who or what controls the wind? Is it some invisible yet infallible force, which makes the wind blow however, and whenever he or she feels the urge? Are increasingly stronger and more frequent winds caused by man-made climate change, which makes us the entity controlling which way the wind blows, whether or not we're cognizant of the ability? Are there other times we cede control, when really we not only control every aspect, but created the design? The ingrained fallacy of going whichever way the wind blows, reveals even more layers when we realize we do have control, but are apathetic and complacent. The first step in our collective evolution is not only discovering that we control the wind, but that we are the wind. Thinking for ourselves can be hard, but gets easier with practice." ☺

FROM THE MIND OF CRITIC SEPTEMBER 19TH 2017

From the mind of critic: "If we're relaxing our day away but hear a knock at the door, do we open it without a second thought? Do we look through the peephole to make sure it's not an armed crazy? Do we move with hesitancy because of no peephole? Do we continue leaving our feet up until the person stops knocking, and stops interrupting our chi? Does the door knock wake us from a sound sleep, making us question whether it's a dream or reality? Being open to opportunities, does not mean being a doormat. We're bombarded constantly with things we should be doing or experiencing, cascading over us whether we're prepared or not. Once we realize being open is vital in acknowledging opportunities, but filtering out the bad and keeping the good is crucial in proving viability, we'll see we have to answer whenever opportunity knocks, specifically to have a chance at building ourselves up. An unexpected guest may roust us from slumber, but they also may be the answer we've been looking for." ☺

FROM THE MIND OF CRITIC SEPTEMBER 20TH 2017

From the mind of critic: "If we don't just talk the talk but walk the walk, while saying do as I say not as I do, are we trying to cover our ass? Is plausible deniability the only path toward success our system allows? If we tell kids they must take actions if they talk, but then tell them to only pay attention to our words not our actions, is it any wonder this generation is taking longer to move forward? Without talk, actions don't mean a damn thing. Maybe that's it, actions and words have much less effect by themselves, but whose power is exponentially magnified when working off each other. Once we realize words and actions are more powerful when working in symbiosis, we'll see we as human beings, are way more powerful when we work together than separately. We can affect much more positive change, when we don't get hung up on one word or action, but on the entire human psyche. Once we view each other as people, we'll not only be talking the talk and walking the walk, but we'll tell everybody they should do as we say and as we do." ☺

FROM THE MIND OF CRITIC SEPTEMBER 21ST 2017

From the mind of critic: "If great things happen when we least expect them, do terrible things happen when we do expect them? Do good things happen when we half expect them, and half not? If we have no expectations, how do we know when to strive toward? Knowing, figuring out and moving forward is hard enough, without expecting something to happen. Maybe the idea is building up our soul and light energy so high, we can't help but share it with others so they can build themselves up. Once we realize expectations are based on what's in our head, instead of the reality on the ground, we'll see that letting go of outcomes dis-assembles the biggest roadblock to our enlightenment. Whether it's finding success, or finding the heart connection that makes our soul sing, great things will only happen if we're open to them, not expecting them." ☺

FROM THE MIND OF CRITIC SEPTEMBER 22ND 2017

From the mind of critic: "If two cultures are historical enemies, do newer generations know why? Are the stories they're told the truth, or a subjective attempt to subvert critical thought? Do groups who have engaged in conflict for centuries want peace? Are they cynical of its success because of countless failures? Does blazing a new trail require destruction of paths to nowhere? Whether it's a culture who has achieved its own country after many wars, or a culture still fighting for one, everybody wants to live in peace. Worn out clichés only disappear, when we stop placing our faith in them. Once we see each other in ourselves, we'll realize that whether somebody is Israeli or Palestinian, Indian or Pakistani, Sunni or Shiite, Hmong, Kurd, Catalan, Roma, Rohinga or others dying to breathe free, conflict only exists because we say it does. Violence and darkness is replaced by peace and love, once we realize that when we kill each other, we're really killing ourselves." ☺

FROM THE MIND OF CRITIC SEPTEMBER 23RD 2017

From the mind of critic: "If we don't see the forest for the trees, do we hate the player and not the game? Do we feel the player is guilty, because they make up the game? Do we feel the game is at fault, because it requires people to be players just to survive? If we don't hate players or games, and can see the forest and all the trees, have we accepted love, peace, kindness and gratitude as concepts to live by? There might be less forests of trees these days, but there are way more players and games than at any point in history. It can be hard to differentiate between what's fake and trying to tear us down, and what's real and trying to build us up. Once we realize knowing ourselves involves erecting filters to let good things in while blocking hurtful ones, we'll see if we consciously make our soul sing, we'll belt out opera quality melodies. It's not about hating the player or the game, it's about deleting hate from our vocabulary, and reigniting the love and kindness we may have ignored. What will we be thankful for, love or hate? What will help us consciously evolve?" ☺

FROM THE MIND OF CRITIC SEPTEMBER 26TH 2017

From the mind of critic: "In a world of micro-climates, how do we prepare for anything, when we have to prepare for everything? Do we over strategize, and come up with every variable we believe could happen? Are we so overwhelmed we don't plan at all, because we don't believe anything will happen? Do we believe extremes are the only way to express true emotions, because our greatest fear isn't being wrong, but wishy-washy? Expecting the unexpected is like not looking for something, when we're looking for something. We can't just turn off emotions like a light switch, but we can use a dimmer, the same with life. Preparation helps, but it doesn't negate action. Once we realize handling life's micro-climates isn't about over or under preparing, but being open to what's in front of our face, we'll see true success means recognizing life's moments for what they are, then moving forward to keep the flow going. Being open means not being closed. Like .38 special said, hold on loosely, but don't let go."☺

FROM THE MIND OF CRITIC SEPTEMBER 27TH 2017

From the mind of critic: "If we separate the environment from the economy, can we save either? If we separate security from freedom, can we have either? If we separate human rights from Black, Latin, Old, Young, Women's, LGBTQ, Poor and Immigrant rights, can we achieve any? If we separate individual needs from that of the group, will we be able to evolve? United we stand, divided we fall is a universal norm, something everybody has said from presidents to Pink Floyd. We all have needs, wants, goals and dreams, and we all want to breathe free. We run into trouble when we think our cause, is more important than somebody else's. Once we realize all of our causes deserve attention, but will only be solved when we see how they interconnect, we'll see that what "we're only successful when we're all successful" really means, is being perceptive of our collective symbiosis. United we stand, or divided we fall, those are our only choices." ☺

FROM THE MIND OF CRITIC SEPTEMBER 28TH 2017

From the mind of critic: "If we think of ourselves as informed consumers, so our money is well spent, do we think of ourselves as informed humans, so our time is well spent? Do we assign the same value to money, as we do time? What do we view as more valuable? We can spend, waste, count, enjoy or create money, which is also the same with time. Neither concept is real. Both only exist as real because we put our faith in them that they're real. Once we realize money and time only control us because we allow them to, we'll see critical thinking gives us the ability to make our own decisions, and the knowledge to know the difference between fleeting happiness and long term joy. We can spend money, and we can spend time. We just have to ask ourselves, what's more important, outer happiness or inner joy? Only our soul knows the answer." ☺

FROM THE MIND OF CRITIC SEPTEMBER 30TH 2017

From the mind of critic: "If the payoff is never as big as the hype, why do we buy in? Do we put more faith into what is, or what could be? Do we know we're setting ourselves up for disappointment, but move forward anyway? Do we believe this might be one of those anomalies we've heard about, but have never seen in practice? We've all heard the cliché, "expect the worse so we don't get disappointed". Where we go wrong is always expecting bad things to happen. So not only are we unprepared for good things to happen, but aren't set up to sustain them either because we don't believe they're real. Once we realize life becomes more balanced when we stop expecting and start accepting, we'll see not only our attitude becomes more positive, but our perceptions will discover that good things can, and do happen. When we see payoffs and hype for the false pictures they paint, the true beauty of the world appears." ☺

FROM THE MIND OF CRITIC OCTOBER 3RD 2017

From the mind of critic: "If the JFK'S eternal flame is meant to burn forever, what fuels the fire? Does piped in gas fuel the flame, like a home fireplace? Does truth, justice, humanism and accountability fuel the flame, like a human who has found their true home? Does the physical manifestation of a philosophical concept help explain the unexplainable, or does it fog over real meaning, as we become lost in a sea of confusion? The ideals JFK and the whole Kennedy family stood for, stands in stark contrast to our current leader. Just how Trump is far from perfect, the Kennedy's weren't perfect either. Are human imperfections represented by the eternal flame, or the will to overcome adversity, or does the flame simply represent a simpler time? Gas might fuel the physical flame, but humanity fuels the reason the flame was lit in the first place. If we forget why or how our eternal flame of humanity burns, it'll surely be extinguished. If we remember our humanity and practice it on a daily basis, it'll remain lit through any weather or government. How eternal our flame is, has always been up to us." ☺

FROM THE MIND OF CRITIC OCTOBER 4TH 2017

From the mind of critic: "If our spiritual journey is a solo mission of understanding and consciousness, do we shy away because we fear being lonely for the rest of our lives? If we're scared of being alone, but know we must be to gain enlightenment, in what direction do we take our first step? If we understand the value of knowing thyself and our alone time, but don't want to be alone forever, how do we balance self-reflection with loving and conscious human interaction? Balancing alone time with human time can be difficult, considering we can't control people's actions. Sometimes we need to be alone but can't, and sometimes we need company, but aren't able. Once we realize all we can control is our reactions and the love we exude, we'll see the more love we put out, the more we get back. Being spiritually enlightened can be lonely, like nobody understands and nobody will love us the way we are. When this thinking becomes ingrained, it closes the door. Will anybody walk through our door, who knows, but they're guaranteed to find somebody else's if ours features a closed sign." ☺

FROM THE MIND OF CRITIC OCTOBER 5TH 2017

From the mind of critic: "If we've continuously kicked the can down the road, are we surprised all the discomfort we avoided has returned to cause us major harm? Have we developed immunity to general population issues, because out of sight, out of mind? Do we know the intelligence we used to avoid glaring realities, caused collective ignorance to rise so high, that few saw the decades long build up to our current predicament? We can all ask how we got here till we're blue in the face, but deep down we know. Those times when we sneered or made a comment about a fellow human not living up to our standards, led us here. When we ignored people pleading for peace, truth and justice, because we said their claims were false when we knew they were true, led us here. When we lashed out, because of jealousy over somebody standing up for their beliefs when we were scared, led us here. Once we realize true freedom doesn't tear people down but builds them up, we'll see human rights aren't finite, there are plenty to go around. Kicking the can might have been fun to play when we were kids, but will destroy our very existence if we play it as adults." ☺

FROM THE MIND OF CRITIC OCTOBER 6TH 2017

From the mind of critic: "If we ask what's the matter with Kansas, do we also ask what's the matter with Mississippi, Alabama, Georgia and Tennessee? Do we ask what's the matter with California, New York, Washington and Vermont? Do we ever look in the mirror and ask what's the matter with ourselves? Whether we're rich, poor, light skinned, dark skinned, college educated or a high school dropout, we all wonder how somebody could vote against their own interests. How could people be poor and working class, yet vote for candidates and policies which benefit only the rich, believing progress will trickle down because the market spreads wealth. Once we realize trickle-down economics has never worked, because rich people hang onto their wealth, we'll see if we're poor, our problem isn't other poor people; it's the people keeping us poor. What's the matter with Kansas, is exactly what's wrong with us. Once we stop separating race and class, we'll stop separating ourselves." ☺

FROM THE MIND OF CRITIC OCTOBER 7TH 2017

From the mind of critic: "If we have to inhale specifically so we can exhale in the physical world, must we do the same in the mental world? Must we do for ourselves, specifically so we can do for others, by inhaling beauty, and exhaling kindness and gratitude? If we ignore others so we can do more for ourselves, does it provide short term gain instead of long term survival? My mom has taught me many things over the years, none as important as remembering to fill my own cup. Basically, if we go around all day filling everybody else's cup, we'll have nothing left for ourselves. Before we expend energy, we have to build energy. Once we realize that to build positive energy, all we have to do is walk outside and breathe in how beautiful the world really is, we'll see keeping balance is a lot easier when we get out of our own way. Inhaling oxygen and exhaling co2 might help us survive, but breathing in beauty and breathing out love, humanism and accountability, is how we allow our species to consciously evolve."☺

FROM THE MIND OF CRITIC OCTOBER 10TH 2017

From the mind of critic: "If everything happens for a reason, yet unreasonable people abound, is it any wonder we try forcing things to happen? Would it change anything if we untethered ourselves from outcomes? Can unreasonable people be reasoned with, or are they a lost cause? Is the concept of a lost cause itself unreasonable, because reasons aren't being identified, even though lost causes have a reason by definition? There are as many cures for laziness, as there are motivations to get out of bed in the morning. Many of them come from meaning what we say, and by doing what we say, not by telling others to do as we say and not as we do. Once we realize not forcing life to happen, but setting up our environment and mind to usher in opportunities is how to be successful, we'll see we're all unreasonable sometimes, but the quicker we realize it, the quicker we become reasonable again. If everything happens for a reason, but we stop looking for that reason because we figure it's easier to force life to appear, it never will." ☺

FROM THE MIND OF CRITIC OCTOBER 11TH 2017

From the mind of critic: "If coastal weather features countless microclimates, shouldn't those microclimates be labeled microcosms? If the weather changes five miles in any direction, and keeps changing in five mile increments as we drive down the road, wouldn't thoughts, feelings, emotions, actions, reactions, beliefs and goals change in the same fashion, and at the same speed? If nothing is as it seems while change is constant, is stability an illusion? The world can be extremely overwhelming, and even more so when we pay attention. The second we have something figured out, something else comes along to prove we have no idea what we're talking about. Once we realize change is inevitable no matter how hard we fight back, we'll see processing infinite microcosms is a fool's errand, but processing how those infinite microcosms make up the exact same macrocosm, is the smartest thing we could ever do. When we discover microcosms and microclimates are the same, is the exact moment we discover all us humans are the same." ☺

FROM THE MIND OF CRITIC OCTOBER 12TH 2017

From the mind of critic: "If our fast food, strip mall, smart phone and big box culture continuously surprise us with its fakeness, have we ever asked why? If we constantly want things to be cheaper, faster and with more variety, but idolize mom and pop businesses, have we ever asked why? The whole reason we get cake is to eat it, right? We all like to talk and talk, but when it comes to action, many of us fail to follow through. If we like quality local food, personal attention, personal interaction and a variety of businesses to choose from, but refuse to pay an extra couple bucks, giant mega corporations who undercut their competitor, will swoop in and fill the void. Once we realize if we're more authentic in our interactions, by talking the talk and walking the walk it leaves us fulfilled, we'll see we always get what we actually need, not what we say we want. We can have mom and pop businesses again if we demand them, and then support them. Big boxes become small boxes, when they lose our support." ☺

FROM THE MIND OF CRITIC OCTOBER 13TH 2017

From the mind of critic: "If guns, god, gays and abortion divide us so much, do we realize it's a learned behavior? Do we realize the gatekeepers want the population divided, because it's easier for them to get away with whatever they want? Do we ever question why we feel the way we feel, or do we just go along because it's the way it has always been? I've probably mentioned it before but it's worth repeating, it all goes back to one of Obama's most mis-characterized phrases. When the media quoted him saying "they cling to their guns and religion", they completely missed the context. Obama said people have been lied to and pushed around for so long, they don't believe any politician. So they cling to their guns and religion, because their emotions are all they have left which hasn't been taken away. Once we realize politicians playing to our emotions cause destruction, and politicians playing to our humanity cause evolution, we'll see the only reason we're being divided, is because the gatekeepers know the power of our unity, and they're scared. Collective unity and humanity always poke through the fog of political division, no matter the thickness. We must remember, united we stand, divided we fall." ☺

FROM THE MIND OF CRITIC OCTOBER 14TH 2017

From the mind of critic: "If we believe cops are never there when we need them, and always when we don't, do we feel safe? If we call the cops when we do need them, and they arrive but say they can't do anything, do we feel safe? If the cops are called on us, when we're guilty of nothing more than being the wrong skin color in the wrong place at the wrong time, do we feel safe? Are the people parroting that we need to give up rights for security, in such a supremacist position that they've never been threatened, because they're the ones taking rights from others? We fix our most ingrained and complex issues, by fixing ourselves. We fix ourselves by looking in the mirror, and realizing the human form staring back is the same human form as everybody else. We stop being scared of the "other", when we stop being scared of ourselves." ☺

FROM THE MIND OF CRITIC OCTOBER 17TH 2017

From the mind of critic: "If we read the directions when all else fails, what do we do when we fail over and over, because there are no directions? Do we flail around, doing the first thing which pops into our head? Do we analyze why we failed, so we can figure out how to succeed? Have we grown so used to following directions, that we don't know how to lead? They say there are three types of people in the world, leaders, followers and get out of the wayers. The comparison misses the point, because we have all three traits within us by virtue of being human. We must be all three in certain situations. We must also not be afraid to read directions when we don't know something, or be so reliant upon directions, the concept of blazing our own trail is a foreign language. Once we realize keeping life in balance is the biggest way to keep our sanity, we'll see whether directions exist or not, if we aren't afraid to exit our comfort zone, we'll never fail. Critical thought is the secret to a fulfilling life." ☺

FROM THE MIND OF CRITIC OCTOBER 18TH 2017

From the mind of critic: "If children's stories and nursery rhymes were too dark and violent back when, and to disney-fied now, where's the happy medium? How do we keep kids innocent as long as possible, while not lying about how the world really is so they become well-adjusted adults? If we teach our kids the difference between real and make believe, the first time they wake at the crack of dawn for Saturday morning cartoons, do we authentically understand the concept? Is it another way of vocalizing do as I say, not as I do? The messages in our kids stories used to reflect the crushing harshness of life, they showed an unvarnished truth; which although dark, was real. Now as an over compensation, we have Disney, DreamWorks, Cartoon Network and countless others which show such a fantastical view, that unless we specifically define real life, our kids will grow up living in a completely unaccountable and gullible fantasy world. Once we realize to teach truth, we have to learn it and then know it, we'll see if the next generation has any hope for a better future, it'll be because we allowed them to indulge their imaginations; while simultaneously letting them know the sometimes dark and ugly, but also light and beautiful truth. The balance between fantasy and truth is achieved, when we realize that to understand one, we have to understand the other." ☺

FROM THE MIND OF CRITIC OCTOBER 19TH 2017

From the mind of critic: "If what doesn't kill us makes us stronger, and we endure many near death experiences, are we the strongest person alive? Does this incubated thick skin, make us more joyful? Does succeeding over adversity, persecution and racism guarantee emotional strength? Do self-inflicted roadblocks provide more learning experiences, than roadblocks inflicted externally? Does changing our reaction to an event give us strength? Many of us have been told we have to trudge through the bad stuff, to reach the good stuff; that to be truly grateful for what we have, we must see how bad things can get. All of us are reached in different ways. Some of us need gory, extreme details, just to find the middle. Some of us need to feel love and support to propel achievement. Once we realize loneliness can't bring us love, and racism can't bring us unity, we'll see it's not the actions we have no control over which steer our destiny, it's our reactions to darkness which drives us toward the light. Knowing what inner darkness feels like is the first step, in not allowing ourselves to go there." ☺

FROM THE MIND OF CRITIC OCTOBER 20TH 2017

From the mind of critic: "If rainbows are caused by dark storm clouds hitting sunlight, is new understanding achieved through honest conflict? If both sides authentically convey their beliefs while showing respect, understanding and humanity as the other side authentically portrays theirs, is positive resolution guaranteed? If things can't be guaranteed, but show a great chance of success through conscious effort, is it the best we can hope for? Compromise isn't a dirty word, and neither is Liberal, Conservative, Republican or Democrat. Labels are based on misconceptions which attempt to alleviate misunderstanding. This misunderstanding can turn into something beautiful, if humanity, kindness and accountability are allowed to enter into honest conversation. Once we realize success is never guaranteed, and all we can do is put ourselves in a place with better odds, we'll see compromise isn't a dirty word; and in fact is one of the most beautiful, because it shows diametrically opposed sides humanely working together. Dark clouds and sunlight might be opposites, but rainbows show the beauty of unity." ☺

FROM THE MIND OF CRITIC OCTOBER 21ST 2017

From the mind of critic: "If human characteristics placed on animals help us better understand them, do animal characteristics placed on humans help us better understand ourselves? Does this better understanding lead to conscious evolution, or further cementing of ingrained attitudes and actions? If we're all animals but supposedly civilized, does learning of our inherent incivility, make us want to turn back the clock, or wind it forward? As we continue understanding animal life by any means necessary, so too must we understand human life by any means necessary. However because of free will, just having the information to help us understand, doesn't guarantee we will. We can take in and use this new understanding, ignore it or we can simply stare blankly. Once we realize animal and human comparisons help explain light, love, dark and hateful actions, we'll see it's up to us to use learned information to better life for humans, by bettering life for all humans. Unity never has and never will fall in our laps. We're all animals and we're all humans, our dominant trait is up to us." ☺

FROM THE MIND OF CRITIC OCTOBER 24TH 2017

From the mind of critic: "If every morning starts a new day, is it a physical start or something more? If every night ends a new day, is it a physical end or something more? Is this beginning and ending cycle a once in a lifetime thing, or a daily routine? Is a physical and emotional beginning and end the same, different or symbiotic? The beginning of a journey can be happy, joyful and full of hopes, dreams and goals. On the same token, the end of a journey can be sad, miserable and full of dread, insecurities and regrets. They can be that way, but just like life, once we think we know how it is, we get thrown a curveball to prove we really don't. Once we realize our beginning and end is not the beginning and end, we'll see we have many beginnings and ends, specifically to clear out old experiences, so we have room for better and more fulfilling ones. Beginnings and ends aren't a start or stop, but a continuous montage of moments, which need constant recognition and clearing out to flow freely." ☺

FROM THE MIND OF CRITIC OCTOBER 25TH 2017

From the mind of critic: "If fog impairs our morning drive, how does some light burn through the fog, while other light magnifies it? Is the brightness of the sun burning off the fog, equal to the brightness of high beams reflecting back? Is it about finding the goldilocks zone, where it's not too bright or dim, but just right? Does shedding to much light make matters worse? The sun is much more powerful than high beam headlights, nobody would deny that. The fog which hangs low these days is and always has been ingrained, with any attempt to shine light on the truth, is seen as fake depending on the news outlet. Sometimes the truth is so different from everything we've heard, it would flip our world upside down to hear anything which questions our outlook. Once we realize the fog which overshadows humanity is the same for all of us, just like the light which illuminates our humanity, we'll see each of us are more likely to internalize truth, if we express it in a humanistic and accountable way. If we talk to somebody instead of at them, they're much more likely to listen. Bright headlights might make fog worse, but humanistic truth, always cuts through. If we have the power to create the fog, we certainly have the power to burn it off. Are we ready to accept a new day?" ☺

FROM THE MIND OF CRITIC OCTOBER 26TH 2017

From the mind of critic: "If ignorance is bliss, is knowledge misery? Does not knowing things make us joyful, because we're ignoring what's blatantly obvious? Does learning the nature of harsh realities make us sad, because we're internalizing how bad some people have it? Does fantasy and reality coexist, or are they one in the same? When we learn something, we can't unlearn it. Once we open that door, it's permanently held open by a doorstop created by our world being flipped. We can close our eyes and pretend our fellow humans aren't hurting, but just because we ignore something, doesn't make it disappear. It makes matters worse when ignorance is ingrained and passed down. Whole generations are taught to hate and fear, letting it filter into their lives; causing them to not remember why they were supposed to hate and fear in the first place. They're so used to ignoring, that they don't view the targets of their venom as having the same human frailties. Once we realize the foundation of bliss is ignoring everything around us, we'll see our inner joy as fake if it tears anybody down. Learning the actual nature of our world can be daunting, but we ensure real joy by learning, then acting. Knowledge only brings misery, if it isn't followed by conscious action." ☺

FROM THE MIND OF CRITIC OCTOBER 27TH 2017

From the mind of critic: "If we care more about a political party than certain issues, do issues really matter? If we care more about certain issues than a political party, do political parties really matter? Do we vote for issues which matter to us, or for a candidate we don't fully support, but is better than the alternative? When somebody is considered an issues voter, they're described as only voting because of certain issues, while ignoring others. If somebody from an opposing party supports issues they care about, they'll vote against; which makes one wonder why we even have political parties. If somebody ran on issues they cared about, people would support them. They could raise money and build a following. There comes a time when we must ask, are political parties used to further a power structure's control, which has been tightening it's iron grip for thousands of years? There also comes a time when we must stand up for what's right, even if it's hard; especially if it's hard. Laziness can't be an excuse for inaction. If we support people, we must support all people. Once we do, the need for political parties will fade. Then, and only then will we have true unity." ☺

FROM THE MIND OF CRITIC OCTOBER 28TH 2017

From the mind of critic: "If we argue racial equality has never fully been achieved, could we also argue we've never really asked why? Have some people asked, while others gloss over the surface? Has a portion of the population been inundated by generations of imbedded racism in advertisements, business, government, family and friends, that things are what they are, and "those people" are like that, so we have to protect "our kind?" We've gotten so used to kicking the can down the road, we've forgotten how to look in the mirror. By being so afraid to deal with our past, let alone admit atrocities, we've allowed problems to fester, because we believe half-ass token responses are good enough. So let me be as clear, and concise as my 36 year old conscious mind will allow. I love America, and all the freedom, equality, peace and justice it's supposed to stand for. However, until we acknowledge our dark, racist, genocidal and ignorant past, and comprehend how it's filtered into our current environment, we will only know token unity. To collectively evolve we must do more than utter platitudes, we must act." ☺

FROM THE MIND OF CRITIC OCTOBER 31ST 2017

From the mind of critic: "If objects, people and events bend to our will, does too the moral arc of the universe? Does the arc always bend toward justice, with our species either shortening or lengthening the bend? Can our thoughts, feelings and actions change the bend to a straight line, or an S curve? Do semantics solve anything, or are they meant to make ourselves feel like we're taking action? Any one of us can change the trajectory of the status quo, society and collective evolution. It may take a while, but chances are if we're determined and passionate enough, people will be drawn toward us, which is where the "we", as in "all of us" comes in. Some of us believe light will win out, and some believe dark will. Once we realize most humans want peace, justice, respect and love, we'll see not only that we succeed when all of us do, but we can bend, straighten, curve or downright destroy the moral arc, depending on who it benefits and who it tears down. Considering we build each other up because we've built ourselves up, we can always shorten or lengthen the road toward justice. What is more beneficial? If our justice takes away justice from others, it's not justice, its tyranny. We all want to fight against tyranny, right?" ☺

FROM THE MIND OF CRITIC NOVEMBER 1ST 2017

From the mind of critic: "If a celebrity we've always admired and respected turns out to be a monster, after an accuser tells their story, what do we do? If our favorite actors define not who we are, but what we use as comparison for other pieces of art, but the actor is a proven child-raper, what do we do? Does power and money always corrupt, or is it a case by case basis? The way some people felt about Bill Cosby when allegations surfaced, is the same way I feel about Kevin Spacey. What the fuck man, seriously? Usual Suspects, American Beauty, House of Cards and many other TV shows and movies, I can't bring myself to watch them anymore. This may sound like a first world problem, to watch an idol fall from grace; of course not nearly as big a problem as for the 14 year old boy he forced himself on. If anything good can be gleaned, it's that this shit won't be tolerated anymore. I will never willfully watch anything with him again. Not all celebrities are rapists and pedophiles right? Oh yeah, and fuck Kevin Spacey, he gives real actors a bad name. He needs to be put in gen-pop somewhere, so he can get a personal tour of what's done to child rapers in prison. It is possible to make it in Hollywood and not be a sexual criminal, right?" ☺

FROM THE MIND OF CRITIC NOVEMBER 2ND 2017

From the mind of critic: If conspiracy theories spawn from a chaotic world, do they disappear in a peaceful world? Do we stop thinking about all the ways the world can get us, when we see black and white benefits? Is the key to handling it all, not to let somebody do all the thinking for us, but for us to think for ourselves? Sometimes we have to think hard to make sense of the world. Sometimes we think too much, and sometimes we don't think at all. Finding balance includes taking a case by case approach, and not trying to apply or expect a one size fits all answer. There's a lot of corruption and criminality underway, and they aren't theories, but cold hard facts. When we stop taking the easy way out by looking for the easy answer, authenticity will appear, and our path forward will illuminate. Translating chaos, breeds more chaos. Translating truth, breeds more truth." ☺

FROM THE MIND OF CRITIC NOVEMBER 3RD 2017

From the mind of critic: "If labels help us make sense of a chaotic world, but inhibit our personal evolution by making us less human, where's the middle ground? Is there a way to label something so we better our understanding, as opposed to deepening our ignorance? Are labels ever objective? The act of labeling like life is dependent on intent. If somebody wants to insult, persecute, belittle and dehumanize somebody else, they usually label them. That way they know what to avoid, and what to claim vast knowledge of, even though actual knowledge is nil. However, if somebody wants to admire, support, build up and love somebody else, they can also label them. This is the act of trying to put words to the vast power of their awesomeness. Once we realize the road to hell is only paved with good intentions, when conscious action isn't a blip on our radar, we'll see actions and words make a complete human being, not either or. Whatever path we take to gain better understanding is a good thing. However, if our intent is good, but our actions lead away from better understanding, we must take an honest look in the mirror." ☺

FROM THE MIND OF CRITIC NOVEMBER 4TH 2017

From the mind of critic: "When spelling out the problems of institutional racism, antisemitism, persecution and all degradation of "the other", do vague descriptions instead of detailed accounts, help us get past self-imposed roadblocks? Do we let fear residue from past incidents, color our perspective? When several interactions with somebody from a different race, culture, religion or sexual orientation turns bad, violent or worse, do we then believe "they" are all like that? If racists are ignorant enough to believe a certain group is monolithic, does the group targeted believe that whatever ethnic group the racists belong to, believes monolithically as well? If we know beating back ignorance involves humanization, how come we spew dehumanization to dispel the ignorance of racists? We all know this is a sticky issue, one we all know about, but might be scared to get involved in. Once we realize racism disappears when humanism appears, we'll see vague descriptions and blanket statements feed ignorance on all sides. The world is dark, but the world is also light. We get past generational difficulties, when we voice specifics, not platitudes." ☺

FROM THE MIND OF CRITIC NOVEMBER 10TH 2017

From the mind of critic: "In the parking lot of life, do we all have a spot? Do some of us need truck and trailer parking, while others need only compact? If there are a finite number of spots, are we a defensive enough parker to find a spot outside the designated lot? All of us want to find our spot, a place we belong. Some of us forget critical thinking, when an easy solution doesn't instantly present itself. Others rely on critical thinking, using creativity and knowledge of inner self to find the niche which drives them. Once we realize life won't always hand us easy solutions, we'll see we can find our passion when we stay open to opportunities we didn't expect, and joyful events, people and activities we may have forgotten. Finding a marked spot can make us happy. Creating our own spot can bring us inner joy." ☺

FROM THE MIND OF CRITIC NOVEMBER 11TH 2017

From the mind of critic: "If the calm before the storm is a quiet moment before things get bad, how will we ever be comfortable with peace, if we're always expecting impending doom? If we're not comfortable with chaos, but are familiar with it, do we question the validity of human gestures? If we always expect the worst, are we prepared for something good to come along? Being scared is normal, and so is worrying about being let down. What isn't normal is believing we'll always be let down, because the power to achieve joy and success is out of our control. By washing our hands of personal effort, we're giving ourselves fleeting bits of happiness, because we think we know what's coming. Once we realize that what we expect is usually what happens, we'll see if we always expect the worst, the worst will always show up; specifically because we didn't make one speck of room for something good. A calm before the storm doesn't always mean a storm is coming, it could mean a new and brighter day is here, if we allow ourselves to view the light." ☺

FROM THE MIND OF CRITIC NOVEMBER 14TH 2017

From the mind of critic: "If the art of the deal was one man's blueprint for being on top, did the public know it was step by step instructions to erase humanity, by squashing anybody who stood in the way of personal gain? As popularity grew, did readers realize making themselves the center of the universe instead of their universe, was only possible if they forsook all other humans? Do some of us wish it was the old west or anarchy, while not realizing practical applications? Ignorance describes an unwillingness to learn, or witness what happens outside of one's bubble. If we want people to stop wheeling and dealing us, we have to stop wheeling and dealing them. While Trump's diary of a con man might have struck a chord during the screw everybody but me Reagan 80s, it's that chord which is currently making the beauty of humanity way out of tune. Whether we're dealing or compromising, it's our intent and positive collective action which propels us forward. Our species can be redirected onto the right course, once we compromise not ourselves, but our misconceptions." ☺

FROM THE MIND OF CRITIC NOVEMBER 15TH 2017

From the mind of critic: "If deflection is our only defense when accusers come forward, is guilt imbedded in our brains? Do we believe pointing out others' wrongs, takes attention away from ours? Are we strong enough to point out deflection only happens, because the guilty party knows they're guilty, but believe themselves to be less guilty than their accuser? In this severely divided time, some of us are willing to look past obvious crimes in our sides' politician, because of fear the other is side taking over. This is when we must look in the mirror and ask, if what we're overlooking in "our guy" happened to "the other guy", would we ignore or react harshly? If the answer is ignore, we can't complain politics are broken, when we're wielding the sledgehammer. Deflection is the last resort of a guilty party. Accountability and humanism is how we climb out of the darkness and into the light." ☺

FROM THE MIND OF CRITIC NOVEMBER 16TH 2017

From the mind of critic: "If the greatest things in life are free, are they hard to find, because we can't run down to the corner store for them? Does not having monetary value make something elusive, because it changes its form and location, depending on the person looking? If hard work doesn't guarantee success, will we be okay with never finding what we're looking for, no matter the volume of blood, sweat and tears we expend? Constantly pursuing success in career and love for our soul, can bring loneliness if we never see brighter days ahead. Is there a way to stay motivated, so we achieve success which drives our passion, and love that makes our soul sing? If I knew the answer, I wouldn't presently feel the way I do. What keeps me going is the knowledge that I still want love and success. The only way I'll find it since I haven't yet, is to stay open for that day when it arrives on my doorstep. How do I stay open? I keep putting myself out there, until something comes along. What else am I going to do, sit on my ass and give up; that would be like admitting I'm not worthy, which I definitely am. I'll never give up, I'll never slow down. I just hope one day it leads me to the love and success my soul yearns for. The greatest things in life are free, but not from effort."☺

FROM THE MIND OF CRITIC NOVEMBER 17TH 2017

From the mind of critic: "If all humans need real connection, how come so many of our actions disconnect us? Is it because talking is a lot easier than doing? Do we take part in newer and newer depersonalizing acts because everyone else is, which in some weird way makes us feel connected, even though it's the exact opposite? Do we want human interaction, but expect it to fall into our laps? Do we only want to take in good stuff, without putting anything good back out? As the world gets more personal, the more it gets impersonal. The more we get connected through social media, 24 hours news, Amazon, credit cards, and home delivered groceries, the more we get disconnected for the same reason. Like the balance of life and humanity, we have free will and aren't governed by what technology and society tells us, but how we infuse humanity into ever changing technology and society. Once we realize treating ourselves special, taking care of ourselves and being a good person aren't just for people with extra time on their hands, but all of us, we'll see our humanity is inherent, and will be constantly tested as the world evolves. Once our actions spring from what we want, not what society and technology tell us, we'll finally walk the walk we constantly talk about." ☺

FROM THE MIND OF CRITIC NOVEMBER 18TH 2017

From the mind of critic: "If one of the secrets to life is balance and moderation, how come so many of our actions seek to unbalance and un-moderate? Are we scared of giving up instant gratification and short term happiness, because our low self-esteem won't allow us the courage, stamina and determination required to achieve seemingly insurmountable goals? Are we so lazy from everything being handed to us, that we believe our thoughts and actions are only unbalanced, because everybody else's are unbalanced? The best and brightest path toward authentic peace of mind, is the realization that life is never perfect, and won't always work out as planned. Over-indulgence happens when we hang onto happy moments too long, hard and tight because we think they won't happen again. How we finally found something or somebody that makes us happy, so we want to hit the repeat button over and over and over again. Once we realize how not to death grip happiness, but simply recognize it, we'll see all the beauty of the world continuously flow through us, because we recognize happiness is stagnating, but joy is fluid. Balance and moderation are achieved when we realize we can't control everything that happens, but we can control our reactions. The world can be as dark and/or light as we choose." ☺

FROM THE MIND OF CRITIC NOVEMBER 21ST 2017

From the mind of critic: "If we're all just dust in the wind, what do we do in a sandstorm? Do we duck for cover and hide, letting all the dust and dirt do what it's going to do, except to us? Do we run in the opposite direction, hoping we can out run the dust? Do we keep moving forward knowing the dust will hit us, but will only stop our forward progress if we allow it to? Flight or fight frequency greatly increases, when we realize all of us struggle. We all want to have a good, prosperous and fulfilling life, while taking care of ourselves and our families. Many things, people and events will affect us positively and negatively along our journey. We can't always change what happens, but can always change our reactions. Are we going to spend our lives running from negativity, endlessly floating from place to place, while telling ourselves we're looking for something, but aren't ready to find it even if we did? Are we going to take a stand, find our passion, place and purpose, and move forward? Sandstorms can grind us down to a nub, but only if we don't know who we are, what we want and what mark we want to leave." ☺

FROM THE MIND OF CRITIC NOVEMBER 22ND 2017

From the mind of critic: "If what about-ism is how we respond to accusations, are we responsible for anything? If we think total control is the only control, are we controlling anything? If we believe we're never at fault, are we admitting to being pawns? We all know black and white denials are usually an explicit admission of guilt, because we're trying to prove something to ourselves beyond a reasonable doubt, while knowing it's the complete opposite. Getting over ourselves is how we evolve. The first step is admitting we're not perfect, being human means being fallible. If blaming accusers is our default solution, we'll forever be stuck in a cycle of low self-esteem on the inside, and sad clown on the outside. If our true goal in life is joy and fulfillment, taking responsibility for our actions is how we get there." ☺

FROM THE MIND OF CRITIC NOVEMBER 23RD 2017

From the mind of critic: "If we create our own realities by learning or not learning from life's experiences, how do we prepare our mind, body and soul for the best possible outcomes? Do we open up to everyone and everything by looking outward, deleting the words "no" and "can't" from our vocabulary? Do we close up to everyone and everything by looking inward, deleting the words "yes" and "can" from our vocabulary? Do we find a happy medium where we're open but with a filter, where we keep the good, lose the bad, and learn lessons so we can keep joy flowing through us? On this day of giving thanks, may we remember the true history and context of the 4th Thursday in November by feeling immense gratitude. Not because we're taking pleasure in others misery and despair, but because we're thankful for what we have. Things can always be better, but they can always be worse. When we strive to bring ourselves joy, specifically so we can bring it to others, we finally understand the true meaning of Thanksgiving. Our realities vis-a-vie our perceptions change for the better, when lessons are learned and adversity is overcome. Staying open means building ourselves up, not tearing ourselves down." ☺

FROM THE MIND OF CRITIC NOVEMBER 24TH 2017

From the mind of critic: "If we know we can agree on 90% of things, but get caught up on the 10% we don't, do we realize it's identical to focusing on our differences, instead of our similarities? Do we believe fighting the hard battles first will get them out of the way, because fighting the easy ones last will provide smooth sailing on the road to tranquility? Do we believe fighting the easy battles first is taking the easy way out, by finding a solution which involves as little work as possible? Making things harder or easier than they need to be, deletes our critical thinking skills. When there are things we must do, starting with the hard and moving into the easy, can be sensible. However, if we're trying to fix complex generational problems, which are only complex because we've made them that way, doing the opposite is how we build sustainable and long lasting change. If we start conversations from the 90% we agree on, then move to the 10% we don't, we'll solve problems much more often. If we talk to each other like humans, we'll see putting somebody down for being different, is like pointing out the difference between snowflakes, while failing to recognize it's all snow. Starting conversations from the 90% we agree on, gives us a head start in the race for unity." ☺

FROM THE MIND OF CRITIC NOVEMBER 25TH 2017

From the mind of critic: "If fear disappears when we have nothing to lose, does it reappear when we have everything to lose? Does fear permeate all the nooks, crannies and pores of everything and everybody we love, and if we lose it, we're losing part of ourselves? Do we believe fear only permeates because we allow it, knowing worry only makes matters worse? Fear and worry are completely normal, just like love and excitement. Part of the balance of life is being thankful for what we have, because we know it can be taken away any time by infinite variables; which constantly reinvent themselves the second we get a handle on them. Not letting emotions permeate is the key. By not gripping them too tight, we'll recognize what they are. We'll be able to decipher which builds us up, tears us down and stunts our progress. If we want emotions to be real, we have to feel them, and let them teach us what they have to teach us. Recognizing our emotions can be scary, but become an enlightening act when we realize it's another step in our conscious and collective evolution. Fear will never fully disappear, because we always have something to lose. Fear can be shrunk and made much less significant however, simply by feeling gratitude. Don't believe me, just try it; you'll see you have nothing to lose, and everything to gain." ☺

FROM THE MIND OF CRITIC NOVEMBER 28TH 2017

From the mind of critic: "If the object of any business is to crank out as much money as possible, are the employees nothing more than a business expense? Do owners realize employees are integral to making profit, but can easily be replaced because so many are hurting for work, therefore negating the need for humanity in decision making? Do employees know they're integral but easily replaceable, so they refrain from speaking up when wage and labor issues arise? Are people just numbers, when the people at the top only see numbers? Most corporate environments are designed to make money, as are all other businesses. Problems surface when so much profit is squeezed out, that quality suffers. Why does quality suffer? When employees are not viewed as people, but interchangeable robots, living wages, benefits, even simple human kindnesses are seen as unnecessary frills. Once we realize happy employees are more productive, we'll see treating employees like humans make the company more money; which stimulates the economy because employees have more money to spend, and will close the ever widening wealth gap. Capitalism does work as a system, but only when it works for all of us." ☺

FROM THE MIND OF CRITIC NOVEMBER 29TH 2017

From the mind of critic: "For true unity to be achieved, can there be any separation? For us to truly see ourselves as equal to each other, do we have to admit we're different? Do we truly have to respect our differences before we respect our similarities? Do we believe unity is only achieved if we're all identical? While it's true the term unity is subjective, humanity is not. Our view on what unity means can differ depending on our background, and what we've had ingrained. However, that doesn't excuse treating others as inhuman. Once we see each other as having the same basic wants and needs, we'll realize that although we come from different places, with different beliefs, skin tones and opinions, we're all the same by virtue of each having unique experiences. True unity is realizing our differences don't tear us apart, but bring us closer together." ☺

FROM THE MIND OF CRITIC NOVEMBER 30TH 2017

From the mind of critic: "If we know who we are and what we want, is it harder to get? Does the confusion and lack of self-knowledge surrounding most of the population, bleed into our thinking, making us question the authenticity of our character? Does all our hard work, diligence, knowledge and determination to achieve our goals make people notice, and then help us achieve by helping them achieve? Does our loneliness, yearning, longing and hope of finding love and success, hurt our chances because we're blocking opportunities? Does not being completely honest with how we feel, make these feelings worse when they become blatantly obvious? Being honest with ourselves is the first step, being honest about what we want is the second. Putting in the hard work and paying our dues to achieve our dreams is the third. The fourth is tricky, this is the step where other people need to help and guide us, because we can't do everything alone. However, sometimes others steer us away and block us from our dreams. The discernment in knowing the difference only comes from being an expert on step one and two. If we want to find love, we can't force somebody to love us. If we want success, we can't force somebody to praise us or buy our product. If we haven't achieved yet but still want to, we guarantee failure by thinking it'll never happen. We achieve by being open and honest, at least I hope so." ☺

FROM THE MIND OF CRITIC DECEMBER 1ST 2017

From the mind of critic: "If life is full of cycles, how do we keep those cycles in balance so we don't run off the road into a ditch? Do we ignore all signs in front of us, which enhance each cycle because we aren't acknowledging their existence? Do we become hyper aware of society, and see what feeds these cycles by over analyzing our actions? Does this over analysis divulge the cycle's design, which inherently puts us out of balance because we're acting not like humans, but robots? Can we figure out how these cycles can be positive or negative, and how we can influence them, without taking away all the joy from life? Learning lessons means being open to something we didn't know before. However, if we delete humanity in favor of scientific theory, we've missed the whole point. Losing weight, bad relationships and job failures all have cycles attached, which catch us in their spokes if we're not paying attention. Success in life, love and joy are also cycles whose spokes can suck us in. There are positive cycles and negative cycles, both can cause us despair by way of apathy and complacency. The way we balance these cycles which balances our life, is self-knowledge through gratitude for everything we have. Building ourselves up and not tearing ourselves down, is how success is born." ☺

FROM THE MIND OF CRITIC DECEMBER 2ND 2017

From the mind of critic: "If we've grown so used to foggy skies blocking light from poking through, do we ignore random light bursts, believing they're phony? Do we only see the light when it's so abundant, it makes us squint? Do we only see light when it's spotty and scattered, believing fog to be so powerful, that if there is a sky full of light it must be a ploy? Do we have the ability to make fog and light more powerful, by how we perceive society? Through our perceptions, we create our own realities. It is through these realities that we reinforce or chip away at built up negativity, which can also be said for positivity. Once we realize the world is only as positive or negative as we choose to view it, we'll see the more positivity we believe is possible, the more will show up. The more light that shows up, the more we'll believe is possible, creating an uplifting cycle we can all achieve. Life is full of choices and possibilities. Light will always build us up, if we allow in its abundant and conscious power." ☺

FROM THE MIND OF CRITIC DECEMBER 5TH 2017

From the mind of critic: "If we want to improve our station in life, do we simply turn the dial? Do we hit the seek button, automatically scrolling through all stations, and stopping on the first clear one? Do we keep tuning the radio until we find not just any station, but the one we're actually looking for? We all want to make our lives better, especially when we see people doing all these great things. We must ask ourselves if we know what we're looking for. Are we looking for any great thing, or our great thing? Once we realize the first step in improving our station is finding what that station is, we'll see that until we find our passion, we'll glom onto any opportunity that brings us fleeting happiness, instead of the long term joy we're seeking. We can improve our station, when we find our passion. We do that, when we stop hitting the seek button." ☺

FROM THE MIND OF CRITIC DECEMBER 6TH 2017

From the mind of critic: "If holiday spirit causes our actions to ooze humanity, have we ever wondered why? Do we think of family, because we want to be close to them? Do we believe nobody wants to feel unloved, because we sure don't? Do we give to the poor, because nobody should go without, or freeze their butt off this time of year? Do we smile more, wave more, love more, sing more and care more? If all great things that make us human are heightened this time of year, we must ask why. If we ask ourselves that honestly, we'll get an honest answer. Once we have that honest answer, we'll see that the only thing stopping us from having that warm feeling all year is us. Whether it's Christmas, Hanukkah, Kwanzaa, Festivus, something else or nothing at all, we're all human and want to be treated as such. The more we remember that, the more problems we'll solve. Which is something we all wish would happen year round." ☺

FROM THE MIND OF CRITIC DECEMBER 7TH 2017

From the mind of critic: "If we want to change our lives for the better, do we believe our current position isn't desirable? Do we only want to move forward, because of all the progress we've made so far? Does earning more money, make us think we're more successful? Does this want to make things better, serve to fully define how good we currently have things? Whether it's a better job or a better life, we all want to keep improving, growing and evolving. While we're deciphering which path to take, we must ask ourselves what we value more, time or money? Would we rather make a few more dollars an hour, or have time for family dinners, keep appointments and feed our passions? Melding these concepts is ideal, but doesn't always play out in reality; which brings us back to what we want, need and are looking to get out of life. Being miserable because we don't have time, is never worth a few extra dollars an hour. Feeling gratitude for everything we have is how we grow truly rich. To change our lives for the better, we must evolve with our passion, not in spite of it. Money brings fleeting happiness, time brings inner joy when we use it to feed our soul." ☺

FROM THE MIND OF CRITIC DECEMBER 8TH 2017

From the mind of critic: "If blinds are meant to deflect light or block it all together, what do we do if they're broken? Do we hang a sheet as a temporary fix, knowing it may not work, but at least we're under the illusion it does? Do we go without blinds, using our hand to block the light? Do we not care if the blinds are broken, because the light is going to shine whether we filter it or not? We make many choices in life, none more important than whether to let light in, and at what volume. With how dark the world can seem, light can be hard to see. Politics and religion can block all light or bring it in, depending on our perceptions; which depend on how much light we choose to see. Once we realize we don't have to be blinded by the light, or swallowed by the darkness, we'll see allowing light to shine, only blinds us when we don't use it to benefit ourselves, specifically so we can benefit the planet. Blinds may let light in, but it's our soul which absorbs it." ☺

FROM THE MIND OF CRITIC DECEMBER 12TH 2017

From the mind of critic: "Is there a balance between evolving with the times, and not going whichever way the wind blows? Can we critically think, using our own thoughts and beliefs, while still growing into better people? Can we expect change, but feel grounded in our beliefs? Can we expect the unexpected, while expecting certain things to always happen? Learning, deciphering and knowing who we are and what we think is always a good thing. Not thinking we have to grow any further, is where we go wrong. We don't have all the answers, but we have some, and become joyful when we understand the concept. Teenagers think they know everything. Some adults do as well, proving they haven't grown out of their teenage phase. Once we realize deciphering when to change and when to stay the same depends on treating others how we like to be treated, we'll see putting others down for being different, is a concrete example of fighting against change, when we know change is inevitable. The key to balance, is realizing black and white explanations don't exist."☺

FROM THE MIND OF CRITIC DECEMBER 13TH 2017

From the mind of critic: "If there are many different holidays this time of year, is the reason we celebrate the same? Do we light candles, say prayers, sing songs and make great food for the same reason? Do we gather friends and family to share light for the same reason? Have we convinced ourselves we celebrate for different reasons, because we don't comprehend why we celebrate? If no person is better than another, no holiday is better than another. I may be inundated with Christmas stuff during December, but it's not going to take away my specialness for Hanukkah. Just like somebody celebrating Hanukkah, isn't going to take away from the specialness of Christmas for somebody else. We might recognize different holidays and historical events, and tell different stories, but we celebrate for the same reason. All our religions, belief and non-belief structures are the same at their roots. Treating others like we'd like to be treated, remembering to share, and loving our fellow human being because we're journeying with them, is what we strive for in our personal lives, as well as our religious or non-religious lives. The sooner we realize that, the sooner we can celebrate together. Isn't strong and sustainable unity what we all strive for? We can love each other, when we begin loving ourselves." ☺

FROM THE MIND OF CRITIC DECEMBER 14TH 2017

From the mind of critic: "What do we do when our anger is so hot and sticky, it melts our soul? What happens when our sadness is so cold and icy, it freezes our soul? What do we do when our emptiness is so barren and gaunt, we're a distant reflection of our former selves? Do we refrain from action whatsoever, so we can curl up in a cocoon? Do we continue losing ourselves a little more each day, simply so we can pay our bills and survive? Do we dig ourselves deeper and deeper, as the paycheck writers grow richer and richer? We all have to work. We all have to do our part. What we don't have to do, is be treated as inhuman. I realize businesses and corporations have profits to worry about, along with bills, insurance and remodeling. What many of them miss is the human factor, the exact thing that makes them money. When employees are thought of as commodities and not living breathing humans, they become less happy, less willing to go the extra mile, and much less productive. What compounds matters even more, is when we're used to receiving human treatment, only to have it ripped away due to ownership change. This makes us question everything, like why the hell am I still here. This emotional roller coaster can break us, and can shrink our soul until we're an empty shell. Getting rid of anger, sadness, and emptiness means gathering joy, this means we have to make changes, no matter how uncomfortable they may be. We start bringing in joy, when we stop bringing ourselves misery." ☺

FROM THE MIND OF CRITIC DECEMBER 15TH 2017

From the mind of critic: "If we are what we eat, are we what we do, act, think and believe? Does each aspect of our personality define us, making it hard to find a black and white definition? Do we define each aspect of our personality, making every moment, thought and event a possible rewriting of preconceptions? Do we say we are what we eat, because saying parts of our personality make up our personality only seems redundant, if we don't think about why? If we complain about things happening, but don't ask why, we've guaranteed they'll happen again, and with greater intensity. Our personalities are formed by our perceptions, which are formed by life experiences, which are formed by the society we've created. If we want to make positive change, we have to understand what goes into creating an environment where that's a possibility. To lay the foundation for that environment, we must ask critical questions, and be skeptical of easy answers. Our personality is made up of many different parts. If we spend all our time figuring that out, we won't see all the physical, emotional and spiritual benefits of growing and evolving. Getting stuck on the first step prevents us from climbing the ladder." ☺

FROM THE MIND OF CRITIC DECEMBER 16TH 2017

From the mind of critic: "If great power comes with great responsibility, does knowledge? Does learning how and why things happen, require positive action? Is knowledge viewed as power, or just something poor people say to make themselves feel better? Whether we're scared, not scared or oblivious to the world around us, it's still happening. Just because we turn a blind eye to misery and suffering, doesn't bring it to an end. Journey said "The wheel in the sky keeps turning, and we don't know where we'll be tomorrow." However, if we pay attention, we'll receive a rough outline of where we're going, and can gauge our choices accordingly. These choices are our power. Once we realize that whether we view strength as power or knowledge, it skews our choices, we'll see collective good and self-aggrandizement, as the positive negative balance which keeps that big wheel in the sky turning. Our definition of power, determines whether we tear society down or build it up." ☺

FROM THE MIND OF CRITIC DECEMBER 19TH 2017

From the mind of critic: "If Hanukkah is the festival of lights, does it celebrate the oil burning for 8 nights, while sanctifying the ancient rebuilding of the temple? Does it celebrate the light which burns eternally within all of us, no matter how dim we let it get? Does it celebrate oil, by frying latkes in America, and Sufganiyot in Israel? Does it simply celebrate one story among many, which can help teach, guide and advise when we're confused about which path to take? On this 8th and final night of Hanukkah, we all need light more than ever. Dark forces have always tried to further their control, but right now they see an opening for acceleration. As humans we have a choice, we can step into the darkness or step into the light. If we don't choose, we've allowed the person closest to us, or the person with the loudest voice to choose for us. In the end, holidays mean whatever we want them to; with the reasons we celebrate as numerous as drops of water in the ocean. We must always remember the things which matter to us, friends, family, shelter and purpose, are the same things which matter to everybody else. That is the light we celebrate this holiday season. That is why we light candles on Hanukkah. If we want to bring light to the darkness, our light might be from different sources, but it's still light. Isn't that all that matters?"☺

FROM THE MIND OF CRITIC DECEMBER 20TH 2017

From the mind of critic: "If we view everything that happens as just the way the cookie crumbles, did we forget our part in the baking? Do we realize there are ingredients which make cookies not crumble? Do we know using oatmeal or oat bran can change the crumble ratio? Does the temperature we bake our cookies at and for how long, affect how they crumble and in which direction? Is there a difference between raw cookies we can't eat, and overbaked or burnt cookies we can't eat? Winds blow, times change and cookies crumble. We can either flow with changes, or fight against them. What we must not do is lay blame, when we could be taking action. Sometimes life happens beyond our control, but sometimes we've tricked ourselves into thinking we have no control, when really we caused events to happen in the first place. The way we tell the difference, is by being conscious of the moment presently in front of us. Then, we can see what set the groundwork for that moment, so we can give ourselves better odds of success. The concept of "we can't control everything that happens, but can control our reactions," is based on being accountable to ourselves, because it's the only way to be accountable to others. Cookies will always crumble, but they always taste better when we admit we helped bake them." ☺

FROM THE MIND OF CRITIC DECEMBER 21ST 2017

From the mind of critic: "Is being trapped physically, the same as being trapped emotionally or financially? Are physical restraints and cages, the same as being so lonely we'll put up with being mistreated? If we're living paycheck to paycheck do we have to put up with being commodities, who can be tossed aside at the slightest inkling of anything less than 100% obedience? Is the world changing so the people at the top have everything, and the workers get tossed so few crumbs, that we not only beat each other to death to get them, but live in so much fear of being 100% destitute, that we put up with being treated as de-facto indebted servants, just for the luxury of being 90% destitute? We can always change our reactions, even if we can't change reality on the ground. The less of us who stand up and demand better treatment, the more it plays into the hands of those who squeeze juice out of a dried up lemon. We can let fear trap us, planning the rest of our lives around how to get shit on the least, while viewing crumbs as extreme luxury. We can also let fear motivate us to stand up and not only say, "we're as mad as hell and aren't going to take it anymore", but to keep standing, pushing, fighting and loving until things change like we all know they can. Why does the caged bird sing, because nobody will sing for them." ☺

FROM THE MIND OF CRITIC DECEMBER 22ND 2017

From the mind of critic: "If we love winter because it's freezing outside, so we curl up by the fire and stay warm inside, are we trying to compensate? Do we draw in cold from the outside to the point of invitation, while repelling the warm inside to the point of a metaphorical brick wall, regardless of the temperature? Are we accustomed to the cold not because it's beneficial, but because it's usual? Are we cynical of the warmth, because the whole idea of self-assessment scares the shit out of us? Is this simply one more example of holiday thoughts and feelings, which should be spread throughout the year? Fake it till we make it, is a concept that can work to get our minds focused in a fulfilling direction. I say can work, because results in life are never guaranteed. The world can be a cruel place, and actively making it less cruel can be intimidating. Through life experience, perceptions and beliefs, we can see through darkness. We know it's freezing outside and want to be warm but think it not possible. We overcompensate, when we should be putting more effort into emotional representation. Once we believe we deserve to be warm all year, we'll take action to make it happen, which makes others believe they can too. It takes less to warm us during the winter, when we're warm on the inside to begin with. Gratitude is the reason for the season, but only as an example of what should be present year round." ☺

FROM THE MIND OF CRITIC DECEMBER 23RD 2017

From the mind of critic: "If all of us are humans who live, die and struggle to know freedom, how can any of us hate freedom? If human beings aren't meant for bondage and constriction, but freedom and continuous positive evolution, how is it possible for a person to yearn for brutal, dictatorial, tyrannical and despotic rule? Have we convinced ourselves that human nature can change, if we blanket over the truth long enough, that we spew nothing but vileness and lies? Do we believe human nature can evolve or devolve depending on how much positivity or negativity we release, which depends specifically on how much we absorb? As living beings, we never stop changing. Sometimes our self-esteem plunges so low, we believe freedom can only be attained by taking it from others. This is where the "they hate freedom" fallacy comes from. Collective freedom doesn't emerge by pillaging it from others, but by allowing ourselves to understand its true definition. If knowledge is power, love and gratitude are its regulator." ☺

FROM THE MIND OF CRITIC DECEMBER 26TH 2017

From the mind of critic: "If employers always want to hire somebody with experience, but a potential employee can't gain experience because nobody will hire them, how do we fix the problem? Do employees have to wait for that one boss to give them a chance, based on their character, drive and willingness to learn? Do employers have to gamble on somebody, based on their character, drive and willingness to learn? Is life one big catch 22, where we can't win for losing, and the grass is always greener on the other side of the fence? Life is full of givers and takers, to be successful, we must locate the middle. Paying it forward means doing for somebody else, after they've done for us. If anybody has taken a chance on us when they didn't have to, we must be willing to take a chance on somebody else when we don't have to. This concept could be described a million ways, but most succinctly, it means do unto others, as you have would them do unto you. Whether we're paycheck writers or paycheck earners, people will prove themselves if given the chance. We just have to ask ourselves, if we don't give anybody a chance, why would we expect them to take a chance on us? If experience is earned, we should let people earn, but only if they have strong character, drive and a willingness to learn." ☺

FROM THE MIND OF CRITIC DECEMBER 27TH 2017

From the mind of critic: "If we need light to see through the darkness, do we need darkness to see through the light? If we see nothing but light, how do we know it's authentic if there's no darkness mixed in, and vice versa? Is ignorance really bliss, or are we too lazy to find truth? We all want to be prosperous, joyful and purposeful, it's a commonality which binds us. What also binds us together, as well as within ourselves, is looking for easy solutions. Sometimes we trudge through our daily routine, and think it'll always be this way or that. Maybe we see ourselves as always succeeding, and don't see any way we could fail. On the flip side, maybe we see ourselves as always failing, and don't see success ever reaching us. We create our own realities through what we perceive. Things can be great, things can suck, and things can fluctuate so wildly it's hard to keep our feet on the ground. We must remember life is a series of moments, which run the gamut of good, bad and in between, due to environment, culture, background, financial status, and infinitely more variables than we have language for. If we hang on too tightly to these moments, meaning changes from its original intent. We might experience a great moment, but make it bad by thinking it'll be the only one we'll ever have, and vice versa. We can be blinded by the light, or swallowed by the darkness. Pure sight leads to truth, which leads to fulfillment, which is gained by observing what's in front of our face." ☺

FROM THE MIND OF CRITIC DECEMBER 28TH 2017

From the mind of critic: "If we're up a creek without a paddle, are we forced to go whichever way the current takes us? Do we use our hands, legs and anything else we can to paddle against the current? Do we let go and let the current take us, knowing the key to survival and success is adaption and self-esteem? If we're lucky enough to have a paddle, will we get turned around easily because we only have one? Does the material and/or manufacturer determine how fast, slow or controlled we move? Whether we have a paddle or not, do we move with, or against the current? Life can be a fickle beast, immediately changing its speed and forcefulness the moment we have it figured out. What we learn through experience is that it doesn't matter how we move forward, just that we move forward. We either create a paddle, or we procure one, neither way is better than the other, specifically because of our intent. Going against the current or with it, doesn't guarantee success, but if we stay conscious we'll see much effort needs to be exerted to increase our chances of success and fulfillment. Life can steal our paddle, but we evolve when we realize we have the ability to create a new one anytime we want." ☺

FROM THE MIND OF CRITIC DECEMBER 29TH 2017

From the mind of critic: "If we learn from past mistakes, are we guaranteed a better future? If we can't change past mistakes, does recognizing them ensure they aren't made again? Does the promise of a New Year, wipe out the lies and dishonesty of the previous year? Part of changing our reactions instead of attempting to change events, is not changing our past, but living a better future now. That way when the future does arrive, we'll be ready because we refined our reactions within our continued conscious evolution, instead of playing catch up. If we want to keep taking two steps forward and one step back, instead of the other way around, humanism, accountability and kindness must be our focus points; not only for ourselves because that's where it starts, but also for our elected officials, especially for our elected officials. This isn't a liberal or conservative thing, it's a being against corruption, violence and elitism thing. Learning from our past mistakes, also means learning from our present ones so we don't keep making them. We will have that better future, when we stop blinding ourselves." ☺

FROM THE MIND OF CRITIC DECEMBER 30TH 2017

From the mind of critic: "If old movies, TV shows, books and comic books are recycled, repackaged and reintroduced every decade or so, are attitudes, opinions and arguments recycled at the same rate? Do we get so blinded by the struggle to survive, that we don't see the inevitable connections between generations? Does putting more energy into changing laws than people's antiquated views, cause demeaning, bigoted, racist, intolerant and violent rhetoric to pop up, whenever the population gets so complacent and apathetic they think racism has completely disappeared? The argument could be made that all ideas are recycled, because there aren't any new ones; that because everything has been done before, we have no hope for original thought. This is how despotic governments grow their power, by deeming human thought heresy, because the top dog always has the final say. Let's make a pact as humans moving forward into this New Year, that we'll abandon our ignorance, shaming, blaming and scheming, in favor of humanism, accountability and kindness. Not only could it be the start of an evolutionary conversation, but the physical representation of not kicking the can down the road, but opening the can and dealing with its contents. Recycling is a good thing, as long as it moves us forward, and not backward. The opposite of apathy, is consciousness."☺

www.ingramcontent.com/pod-product-compliance
Lightning Source LLC
Chambersburg PA
CBHW032035150426
43194CB00006B/294